Becky Gill

Dramascripts

Heaven and Earth

David Calcutt

Published in 2001 by:
Nelson Thornes Ltd
Delta Place
27 Bath Road
CHELTENHAM
GL53 7TH
United Kingdom

01 02 03 04 05 / 10 9 8 7 6 5 4 3 2 1

A catalogue record for this book is available from the British Library

ISBN 0-7487-6017-2

Illustrations by Jane Taylor
Page make-up by Peter Nickol

Printed and bound in Great Britain by T. J. International

Contents

Series Editor's Introduction

Dramascripts is an exciting series of plays especially chosen for students in lower and middle years of secondary school. The titles range from the best in modern writing to adaptations of classic texts such as *A Christmas Carol* and *Silas Marner*.

Dramascripts can be read or acted purely for the enjoyment and stimulation that they provide; however, each play in the series also offers all the support that pupils need in working with the text in the classroom:

- **Introduction** – this offers important background information and explains something about the ways in which the play came to be written.
- **Script** – this is clearly set out in ways that make the play easy to handle in the classroom.
- **Looking back at the plays** – this section has further activities for more extended work on the play as a whole, with emphasis on characters, plots, themes and language.

John O'Connor

Introduction:
Heaven and Earth

The Mystery Plays

During the Middle Ages, one of the most important festivals in the Christian year was that of Corpus Christi. This feast was celebrated on the Thursday following Trinity Sunday, and occurred in the summer, some time between May 23rd and June 24th. Unlike other feast days, such as Christmas and Easter, the feast didn't commemorate any particular event, but was meant to celebrate the birth, death and resurrection of Christ. Because this was summer and the days were long, many different kinds of festivities could take place, in which everyone could be involved. One of these was the presentation of a series of religious plays.

They probably began by telling the story of the main events of Christ's life, and were performed outside the church; but, over a period of time, the plays grew in number, dramatising stories from both the Old and the New Testaments, beginning with God's creation of the world, and ending with Christ's resurrection and the Last Judgement at the end of the world. This series or cycle of plays was performed throughout the whole town, each play being staged on a large cart, or Pageant, which could be pulled through the streets. No one knows for certain when the first cycle was performed, or where. The first known reference to a performance is in York in the year 1378, though it is thought that the Chester cycle began in 1375.

From that time on, their popularity grew rapidly, and soon many towns and cities across England had their own cycle of plays, created especially for them and presented regularly each year by members of the town's Guilds. They must have been spectacular events, with their brightly decorated stages mounted on massive carts, and their elaborate use of props and costumes. It is known, for example, that actors playing devils performed acrobatics onstage, ran howling through the watching crowd, even carrying lighted fireworks to create the smoke and flames of hell! What's more, everyone who saw these plays, rich and poor alike, could enjoy them, because they were performed in English. This may not seem surprising, until you realise that, up till then, all literature was written in Latin. Poetry, religious texts, legal documents, historical accounts all used the language of the Catholic Church in Rome; at that time, England was very much a part of that Church. All people who could read and write did so chiefly in Latin. It was the language of the educated. But that excluded most of the ordinary people of the country, who could not read and write, and whose everyday language was English. Now, for the first time, work of a serious nature was being written and spoken in the common language of the people.

For the next two hundred years these plays were performed regularly, and they had a massive influence on the development of theatre in England. They were finally suppressed during the Reformation, when England ceased to be a Roman Catholic country, and their last recorded performance is in the year 1576. Interestingly, this is the same year in which the first purpose-built theatre was built in London, and the start of the great flowering of English Elizabethan drama that produced, among others, the works of Christopher Marlowe, Ben Jonson, and William Shakespeare.

Writing *Heaven and Earth*

My main interest in the Mystery Plays is the fact that they mark the beginnings of English drama. They are the bedrock on which theatre in Britain is built. All the themes that are dealt with in plays today are present in the Mystery Plays – love, hate, jealousy, family rivalry, crime and punishment, revenge and forgiveness, comedy, tragedy; they're all there. So I thought it would be interesting to look back at those plays, and to see if I could write a version of some of them – aiming both to give a flavour of what they were originally like, and to speak to a modern twenty-first-century audience.

Only four complete texts survive of the many cycles that were produced during the Middle Ages – those of York, Wakefield, Chester and Coventry. Of these, York has the greatest number of plays: forty-eight. From these I chose eight that I felt best represented the range and diversity of the originals, and that covered the complete cycle from creation to resurrection. What I have then tried to do is use the originals as a kind of blueprint for eight new plays, which cover roughly the same dramatic ground, but approach it in a different way, or present the events in a slightly different light. Again, I wanted the language and voice of the plays to be rooted in that original common tongue of the Middle Ages, but to speak very much in the common tongue of our own time. So, because the originals were written in verse, I also decided to write these in verse – but not always adhering to the strict verse-patterns employed in the originals. I wanted to have a freer hand, to use whatever form of verse I felt was fit and right for a particular character or event. With many of the plays, therefore, you'll find several different verse-forms jostling together within the same play, some of them written in a strict metre, others quite free and without any regular metre or rhyme.

The original Mystery Plays took the bible stories, and from them created fully living dramas for the stage, with plot, characters and dramatic incident, sometimes solemn, sometimes comic, sometimes tragic – dramas that spoke of eternal truths, but set firmly in the time for which they were written. Wanting to do the same thing, I used the original plays as a kind of blueprint for new plays of my own, plays rooted in those originals, but growing out of and sometimes away from them, letting my own imagination take off from where they ended. Some of the plays – such as the one about the Shepherds, follow the original fairly closely. Some, like the play about Mary and Joseph, have moved a long way from the original. But what I've tried to do with all of them is to try and show that these first English dramas can still speak to us now, and be as fresh and moving as when they were first written.

Notes on the individual plays

Rebellion in Heaven
Unlike most of the other plays in the Mystery Cycles, this isn't based on a bible story. I've followed the original version fairly closely, but Lucifer's speech of defiance at the end is derived from the first book of John Milton's epic poem *Paradise Lost*, written in the seventeenth century.

Adam and Eve
This is based on the Adam and Eve plays of the Mystery Cycles. Although it follows the well-known story of the temptation and fall of Adam and Eve, I've completely changed the style in which it is written. I wanted this play to have a kind of folk-tale feel, as if Adam and Eve are remembering something that happened a long time ago, and turning it into a story. I've also made Adam and Eve partners in crime in the eating of the fruit, rather than placing all the blame on Eve, as was done in medieval times.

Cain and Abel
Once again, I kept fairly close to the plot of the original play, with the addition of Eve as an old woman, struggling to survive in the world. The reason for this addition is that I wanted to give a sense of earthy reality to the play, and to fix it firmly in the real, human world. A world-weary, ageing Eve seemed the best character to do this. It also provided another, more personal motive for Cain's crime – jealousy of his mother's favouritism towards Abel, as well as God's. Many of Shakespeare's plays deal with the theme of rivalry between brothers, and I guess their origin can be found here.

The Flood
I saw this play as a kind of miniature epic, hence the division into different parts, the use of many different forms of verse, and the movement back and forth between tragedy and comedy. As I was writing it, in the autumn of the

year 2000, I couldn't help having in mind the storms and floods that were bringing chaos to parts of Britain at that time. Also, because this was the end of the first part of the sequence, I wanted to show a change coming about in God's mind, so that, through human example, he actually becomes more merciful. The idea that God – or whatever name we may give to the spirit of creation – is capable of change and growth, is an important one, I think.

Mary

As with *Rebellion in Heaven* there's no real basis for the story of this play to be found in the Bible. The idea of Joseph being suspicious of Mary's pregnancy seems to be a medieval idea, and this is the subject of the original play. The inclusion of Mary's parents, and the character of her father, is my own invention. I wanted to make this play, as far as possible, a purely human drama, and to keep its 'miraculous' aspect at arm's length. So Mary's speech makes no mention of God or visiting angels, and she interprets what's happened to her in her own way.

The Shepherds

The original of this play is the second Shepherds' Play from the Wakefield Cycle, one of the most inventive and comic of all the Mystery plays. I've hardly changed it at all, apart from modernising the language, and having all the characters speak in blank, or unrhymed verse – the same kind of verse that Shakespeare used in his plays, except that in Shakespeare's plays it's only royalty or characters of high status who speak in blank verse. Here, as a way of giving them their due, I've let these lowly characters speak in this way.

The Slaughter of the Innocents

I've compressed three plays into one here – 'The Flight into Egypt', 'The Slaughter of the Innocents' and 'The Death of Herod'. For me, this is one of the most moving episodes in all the cycles of plays, and the killing of the children is, sadly, an act all too familiar to us today from television news reports.

The Crucifixion and the Resurrection

For the final play in the sequence, I followed in part the York play of the Crucifixion for the characterisation of the soldiers. But I also had to bring in reference to incidents from the plays dealing with Jesus' life – his temptation by Lucifer, the miracles, the death of John the Baptist, the raising of Lazarus, and so on. The two Choruses I borrowed from Ancient Greek drama; they are my own invention in this context, as is the writing of the Resurrection. Normally, the entire cycle finishes with a play called 'The Last Judgement', which shows the end of the world. As this hasn't happened yet, I left it out, but did make a kind of reference to it in God's final speech.

Guilds and Mystery Plays

During the Middle Ages, craft or trade guilds became an important feature of town life. People who worked at various trades or crafts – weavers, bakers, carpenters, wheel-makers, and so on – formed themselves into associations with the aim of giving support and help to each other, a bit like present-day trade unions. Each member would pay in a regular subscription to the guild, and these funds could then be used (for example) to help guild-members who fell sick and couldn't work. Many of the most important guilds became quite rich, and heads of guilds became important and influential people in the development and growth of the town. Leaders of all the town's guilds would meet regularly to discuss guild and town business in a specially constructed building called the Guild Hall. One of the tasks taken on by the guilds was the yearly production of the town's cycle of Mystery Plays at Corpus Christi.

The actors, the director and the prompter were probably provided by the town's church authorities, while the guilds provided the wagons, the staging, costumes, props, and possibly actors for minor roles.

As far as possible, guilds would take on plays that were appropriate to their trade or craft. Here are a few examples:

Noah – The Shipwrights' Guild (building the ark)

The Last Supper – The Bakers' Guild (baking the bread and food for the play)

The Crucifixion – The Pinners' Guild (Pinners made pins and nails)

The Adoration of the Kings – The Goldsmiths' Guild (providing the rich ornaments for the Three Kings)

The staging of the plays, then, became an occasion for each guild to show off its skill, or 'mastery'. Medieval pronunciation of this word sounded more like 'mystery', so the plays became knows as 'Mastery' or 'Mystery' Plays.

If 'Heaven and Earth' was being staged in this way, which trade or craft do you think might have been responsible for the production of each of the plays? Read through one of them, and see if you can think of something important in the production that might be provided or created by a particular trade or craft. You can choose either a medieval or modern trade.

Many towns still have their Guild Halls. If yours has, see what you can find out about it. When was it first built? How long was it in use as a meeting place for the Guilds? When did it stop being used? What is it used for now? If you have a local museum, or local history library, you can probably find out much of the information from there.

David Calcutt

HEAVEN AND EARTH

PART 1 CREATION, FALL AND FLOOD

1 REBELLION IN HEAVEN

Curtains closed:

Complete darkness. From the darkness, a voice cries out.

GOD Let there be light!

The stage is lit, instantly. It is empty, except for a throne, raised above the stage. GOD stands before the throne, and speaks out to the audience.

Behold the universe! Its boundless, endless space!
Behold this wonder-work of fire and ice!
Here all things are that one day are to be,
For all things have beginning within me.
I am the maker, God, creation's king,
I make the planets dance, cause stars to sing.
And here, where all the flames of heaven burn,
The centre round which all creation turns,
Behold my throne, lit by eternal light,
The symbol of my majesty and might.
And all about it, let angels appear,
The guardians and spirits of the spheres.

ANGELS appear on all parts of the stage.

Each one shall have its duty to perform,
To keep my pure creation free from harm.
Each star that burns, each world that spins through space
Shall have its guardian spirit, strong in grace.
And Lucifer, the brightest and the best

Of all these angels, and most loved and blessed,
In him I place all trust, and he alone
Shall be the keeper of my heavenly throne.

LUCIFER approaches GOD.

LUCIFER
Great Deity, it's my delight
To bow beneath your power and might.
To do your will's my one desire,
Bathed in your everlasting fire. 3
And so, to you I bend my knee,
The servant of your Majesty.
And let each one here do the same,
And praise in truth your sacred name.

LUCIFER and all the other ANGELS kneel before GOD.

GOD
Now heaven's course is fixed. My will is done.
Let planets spin, let every star and sun
Burst forth with living flame – for Time's begun!

GOD leaves the stage. LUCIFER stands, and speaks to the audience.

LUCIFER
See how I shine! 4
See how I blaze and burn!
My wings stretch far and wide,
Beneath my feet the planets wheel and ride
And stars keep to their course!
Lucifer is my name,
Lucifer the fire and flame
That illuminates the entire universe!
Why shouldn't I be proud?
Aren't I wondrous sight to see?
I look into the mirror of creation 5
And I see my face alone,
My light the brightest
Of the whole angelic company!
I'll bend my knee
To no false deity!
That celestial seat

Is mine by right!
Hour upon hour
I feel my power grow stronger!
Why should I wait any longer?
I'll ascend this height
And claim that throne
And then I'll rule the universe alone!

He calls.

Lightfoot!

One of the angels comes forward to LUCIFER.

LIGHTFOOT Master, I'm here,
Ready to serve you, without fright or fear.
From this time on you'll be
My one and only deity.

LUCIFER What others recognise my right?

LIGHTFOOT A throng
A thousand strong and more.
Half the might
Of heaven's host.
As for the rest –

LUCIFER They'll learn to serve!
Or get the punishment they deserve!
In some deep, stinking pit
They'll rot,
In blackest fires they'll burn.
And then they'll learn
Who's Master and who's not!

To himself.

And if I doubt
I have the right
To take that throne,
Those doubts I'll cast aside –

For now I've gone so far I can't turn back,
And even though creation cracks 9
Deep and wide
And falls apart,
And though I'm doomed and damned
The worm is in my heart
And I'll go on.

LUCIFER turns and begins to climb up towards the throne.

LIGHTFOOT
He climbs to claim
Creation's chair,
It won't take long,
He's almost there. 10
See how his awesome
Power grows,
See how his body
Gleams and glows
From head to foot,
From wing to tail,
A living flame,
A burning jewel.
Now he's at
The utmost height, 11
He's got that throne
Fixed in his sights!
He reaches up –
Creation jolts!
As if shot through
With lightning bolts!
A thunderous noise
Roars in his ears!
A voice cries out!

GOD
Your God is here! 12

GOD enters and stands above LUCIFER, who crouches near the throne. GOD is accompanied by the three angels MICHAEL, GABRIEL and RAPHAEL.

Down, Lucifer! Back down where you belong!
You have committed a most grievous wrong!
You've reached too high, and now you'll fall as far
As once you rose, heaven's brightest star
Bloated with pride and wicked vanity –
Your beauty now is hideous to me!
You really thought this battle could be won?
The war was lost before it was begun.
Your rebel army's beaten and cast down
Into hell's pit, and there they howl and moan,
Banished for all time from heaven's light
To dwell in darkness and eternal night.

MICHAEL Head and foot they're bound in chains – — Dance throughout speech.

GABRIEL Racked by agonising pains –

RAPHAEL Writhing in tormenting flames.

MICHAEL A lake of fire boils and churns –

GABRIEL Where their bodies twist and turn –

RAPHAEL Blistered, scalded, boiled and burned.

MICHAEL Lost in clouds of sulphurous smoke –

GABRIEL Voices twisted to a croak –

RAPHAEL On their tongues they gag and choke.

MICHAEL This their doom and this their fate –

GABRIEL This the consequence of hate –

RAPHAEL Thrust within hell's burning gate –

MICHAEL Where these words are written clear –

GABRIEL For all to see, and all to fear –

All three speak together.

GABRIEL 'Abandon hope all those who enter here!'

Hell's mouth opens to reveal DEVILS in torment. They cry out:

1ST DEVIL
Why did we fall to be so foul?
Once I could sing, now all I can do is howl!

2ND DEVIL
My body's a wound that will not heal!
My flesh a crawling itch
That I can't scratch!

3RD DEVIL
I rage and wretch!
I grind my teeth!
My arse is on fire
And the flames come out of my mouth!

4TH DEVIL
I'm a burning wire!
See how I'm twisted out of shape!
Wrenched from beauty to this hideous state!

5TH DEVIL
See my jaws gape!
I want to eat!
I'll tear my own flesh with my teeth!

6TH DEVIL
I sting! I smart!
This whole place is one great, foul fart
That stench! That smell!
I curse the day I fell
To writhe in stinking hell!

LIGHTFOOT
The game's all up,
We've lost the war,
My friends have fallen
Deep and far,
And where they've gone
I'll go as well,
And follow them
Down into hell.

LIGHTFOOT leaps into Hell's mouth and joins the other devils. GOD speaks to LUCIFER.

GOD
This is the place of torment and of pain,

This is the dreadful kingdom that you'll reign,
A twisted thing of darkness and cruel hate…
Yet even now you can escape this fate,
If you will only bow and bend your knee,
Repent your crime, accept my sovereignty.

LUCIFER
Submit to you?
That I'll never do!
Lucifer is my name,
I am what I am
And so I shall remain
Your sworn enemy
For all eternity.
For I hate you and all of your creation!
And so I'll go down grinning to damnation!

GOD speaks to the three ANGELS.

GOD
Michael, Gabriel, and you, Raphael,
Grant him his wish – and cast him into hell.

The three angels take hold of LUCIFER.

MICHAEL
Down you go to dark and gloom!

GABRIEL
Imprisoned in hell's living tomb!

RAPHAEL
Lord of darkness, king of doom!

They throw LUCIFER down into Hell's mouth. He speaks to the other DEVILS.

LUCIFER
Behold hell's deep!
Behold this fiery chasm where flames creep
And twist and curl!
See this hole where we've been hurled
To writhe in pain!
Once we were bright and fair!
Once we were kings of light and air!
But do I despair?
Do I complain?

Observe my grin.
That too is eternal,
As is my hate
For all things heavenly and divine!
And so, rather than rage
Let's turn our fall
To our advantage,
Plot our revenge
To ruin God's creation
And hurl our challenge
To the open sky.
Let heaven hear our defiant cry,
Open up damnation's door.
Yawn wide
Doom's jaws.
Like arrows tipped with hate
Let curses fly
And let hell howl and roar!

Howling and roaring the DEVILS go, leaving LUCIFER alone.

My course is set. Now I'll not rest until
All God has made I've dragged down into hell.

LUCIFER goes.

GOD Creation creaks, corrupted by this crime
That shall reverberate through all of time.
The universe itself now stands condemned
And some cure for its ailment must be found,
An antidote to struggle and to strife,
And so it's my intention to make life.
For life's the true expression of my love,
The power that makes the stars and atoms move.
I'll make a world where life can thrive and bloom,
A flower growing from creation's tomb,
And in that world this life shall multiply,
More numerous than stars are in the sky,
In colour, shape, form and variety,

A hymn to difference and diversity.
And to this act I now bend all my will,
And shall not cease from labouring until
The shining force of every living soul
Has healed the wound, and made creation whole.

GOD and the ANGELS go.

End of the First Play

2 Adam and Eve

The Creation

ADAM and EVE enter.

ADAM Once upon a time –

EVE God created the world.

A chorus of ANGELS enter. They may use mime movement to create some of the images of the things they describe.

ANGELS
First of all, there was just darkness
But a light was hidden inside that darkness
And God found the light inside the darkness
And plucked it out with a finger and thumb
He plucked out the light
And set it free. 1

ADAM He held it in his hand, a globe of light. It grew brighter.

EVE He held it up. And with that light, he peered into the darkness.

ADAM And what did he see there?

EVE He saw water.

ANGELS
Seething and churning!
Heaving and boiling!
Thumping and crashing!
Raging and lashing!
A great storm of water! 2
A vast, rolling ocean!
And God plunged his arms down into the water,
He plunged them in deep, right up to the elbows,
Grabbed hold of the earth and heaved it out!

And there it was with its hills and valleys
Its plants and flowers
Its bushes and trees,
There it was with its mountains and rivers
And the sea wrapped around it like a blue cloak.

ADAM And there was the sun, up in the sky.

EVE And there was the moon, up in the sky.

ADAM Brave, golden sun.

EVE Silver, singing moon.

ADAM Sun for day.

EVE Moon for night.

ADAM Like brother and sister.

EVE Husband and wife.

ADAM He made them both, just like everything else.

EVE Just like he made all the creatures of the earth.

ANGELS The creatures of the ocean
With their jaws and their fins,
The birds of the air
With their songs and their feathers
Their cries and their colours,
The creatures of the earth
With their fur and their scales
Their love and their hunger
And their noses and tails,
God clapped his hands and they all appeared
As if they'd exploded out of that clap.
They came out flying, they came out fighting,
They came out breathing, they came out biting
And leaping and crawling
And scratching and yawning
And slithering and prancing

And diving and dancing,
The birds dancing in the sky,
The fish dancing in the sea,
The animals dancing on the earth,
And even the trees and the rocks and the stones,
All were dancing, the whole earth was dancing
The steps of the dance that God had made.

ADAM And when the dance was done, God felt tired.

EVE So he sat down on the bank of a river.

ADAM And there, on the bank of that river –

EVE He had an idea.

ANGELS He thought he'd make a creature
A new kind of creature
A creature that could think
A creature that could talk
A creature that stood on two legs when it walked.
So he took a handful of red, sticky blood
And made it into bone and flesh and blood
He made one creature, he made two –

ADAM AND EVE He made me, and he made you.

ADAM And we looked around and found ourselves here.

EVE Here, in this garden, that he made for us.

ADAM And God was here too.

EVE And he spoke to us and said –

GOD enters.

GOD This is Eden. Tend it and keep it. From every tree of the garden you may freely eat; but from this tree, which is the tree of the knowledge of good and evil, you shall not eat. For on the day that you eat the fruit of it, you shall surely die.

GOD turns and goes again.

ADAM And then he was gone and we were alone –

EVE And the sun was shining
And the air was sweet –

ADAM And we sat down beneath this tree
And told the tale –

EVE Of how the world and we were made.

The Fall

The SERPENT enters. It approaches ADAM and EVE.

SERPENT And then there came a serpent.

ANGELS Gold-black shining
Amongst dappled grass
Graceful in sunlight
Gliding towards them
Sinewy-smooth
Lithe and long
Supple and strong 10
It stood before them
As if by chance
And they were… entranced.

ADAM and EVE stand and gaze at the serpent.

ADAM Enraptured!

EVE Amazed!

ADAM All of God's created creatures we knew,

EVE But this was like nothing we'd seen before,

ADAM The most beautiful of all God's creatures.

EVE And when it spoke its voice was fair. 11

The SERPENT speaks to ADAM and EVE.

SERPENT One of God's creatures?
I'm not one of God's creatures.
If you think that, you're greatly mistaken.

ADAM and EVE speak to the SERPENT.

ADAM But you must be!

EVE God made everything.

ADAM He made the world.

EVE He made all the creatures in the world.

ADAM He made us.

EVE He must have made you.

SERPENT No God made me.
No God made this world.
The world was here long before God.
I was here long before God.
Listen, I'll tell you the true story,
I'll tell you what really happened.
And I know what really happened
Because I've been here from the very beginning.

ADAM So we listened –

EVE And it told us –

ADAM This strange, beautiful creature –

EVE And this is what it told us.

SERPENT God was not always God.
Once he was a creature, just like you,
Just one of the world's ordinary creatures,
Until one day, when he was hungry
He ate the fruit of that tree.
That tree there, he ate its fruit.
And that's when he became God.
It was that fruit that made him God,
That fruit that made him powerful,
That fruit that gave him knowledge
Of all the secrets of creation.
If you don't believe me, try it yourselves.

ADAM But God told us not to. He was quite clear about it.

EVE 'Eat that fruit,' he said, 'and you'll die.'

SERPENT
Of course he told you that.
I mean, he would, wouldn't he?
He doesn't want any competition. 15
He doesn't want you to be equal with him.
But eat the fruit of that tree and you will be like him,
You'll become like God.
More powerful than God,
Because there are two of you
And only one of him.
Believe me, what I say is true,
I'm being honest with you.
Do I seem like a creature that would tell you lies?
I am old and I am wise. 16
Eat the fruit,
Become lords of land and sea and sky
And all that lies beyond.
One God is bad news:
What we need is choice and variety.
The more gods the better – don't you agree?

ADAM
And that's how it happened –

EVE
And before we even knew just what had happened –

ADAM
Before we realised we'd done it –

EVE
We'd done it! 17

The SERPENT cries out in triumph.

SERPENT
And God's creation fell apart
And everything tumbled down into hell!

The SERPENT leaps down into Hell's mouth. ADAM and EVE cry out in fear and panic.

ANGELS
The air grew dark!
The earth creaked!
A cold wind howled!
Lightning flared and cracked!
And everything was lit by a strange, eerie light. 18

ADAM And we stared at each other in that strange light.

EVE And we stared in horror at what we saw.

ANGELS
They looked at their faces
And saw horrible masks,
They looked at their bodies
And saw bags of flesh,
They looked at their hands
And they saw blood dripping,
They looked at their mouths
And they saw fangs gleaming,
They looked into each other's eyes
And saw black, empty holes,
They looked into each other's hearts
And saw graves in the ground.

ADAM and EVE speak together.

ADAM AND EVE
And beyond our hearts
And beyond our eyes
And beyond our mouths
And beyond our hands
And beyond our bodies
And beyond our faces
And beyond the horror

ADAM We saw God.

EVE And God spoke.

GOD appears, above them.

GOD Behold! You have eaten of the fruit of the tree that I forbade you to eat. For the tree is the tree of the knowledge of good and evil, which is knowledge of death. And in tasting the fruit you have tasted death, and as the fruit was sweet so death shall be bitter. For from this day the earth beneath your feet is cursed, and you are cursed that walk upon it; and all your days you shall know toil and pain, until the time of your death; and then you shall be cast down into the earth; and earth shall fill up your eyes, and shall fill up your mouths, and shall fill up your ears and shall fill up your hearts; and your bodies will be consumed in earth, for from earth you were made and to earth you shall return.

GOD goes.

ADAM They were the last words he spoke to us.

EVE We never heard him again. 22

ADAM We never saw him again.

EVE We were driven out of Eden.

ADAM And we knew we'd never go back there again.

EVE But we'd carry it with us like the memory of a dream –

ADAM As we set our faces to this world –

EVE Where the wind struck cold and sharp –

ADAM And the ground was baked hard beneath a fierce sun –

EVE That rose behind us and threw our shadows across the land –

ADAM And our feet trod where our shadows walked – 23

EVE …the empty roads of our only home.

ADAM and EVE go.

END OF THE SECOND PLAY

3 Cain and Abel

EVE enters, an old woman. She sits and speaks aloud, to herself and the audience.

EVE Oh! My feet! My back! Oh! My legs! My neck! Oh! How my whole body aches with this business of living! How long have I lugged it around this world? Too long for my liking! My joints am all swole, my teeth falling out, I'm half-blind, half-deaf, and I've got a bad leg! What a wearisome, wearing life this has been. Strife and struggle, hardship and heartache! Not to mention the heartburn! When I think of what we was, and what it is we've come down to! How far we've fallen since our leaving of Eden. A worn, haggard wreck of a woman I am. And as for Adam, he's worse off than me. A shadow, a wraith, the ghost of a man. Two weeks ago he took to his bed, too weak to rise, and he hasn't moved since. And he's not in his right mind. His wits have gone. He just lies there, muttering to himself, babbling of trees and rivers and green fields. And angels. He says he can see angels all around him. I've looked and I can't see any. Between me and this ground he's not long for the world. And I don't think he'll be sorry to leave it. I wouldn't be, neither, if it wasn't for my sons. Two good lads they are, Abel and Cain. The only blessing this world's given to me. And I suppose, if I'm honest, I must thank God for them. For they're all that stand between me and utter despair.

ABEL enters. He carries a dead ram across his shoulders.

ABEL Here come I, my dear mother's first son,
And, between you and me, I'm her favourite one.
With my winning looks and my cheery smile
I make all the toils of her life worthwhile.
I'm loving and caring, gentle and mild,
A most considerate, heartwarming child.

Abel's my name, and I'm sure you'll agree,
No mother could have better son than me.

He lays the ram down as CAIN enters, carrying across his shoulders a sheaf of wheat. In his belt there is a small scythe.

CAIN Here come I, the second son born,
With sadness and grief my heart is torn,
For though I try to please as hard as I can,
I'm not only second, but the second-best son.
I'm sullen, suspicious, without charm or grace,
And walk through the world with a frown on my face.
Cain I was named on the day of my birth,
A child full of fury, and lacking in worth.

EVE rises and approaches ABEL and CAIN. She speaks to CAIN.

EVE Cain, you big dafty, you know that's not true,
My love's shared alike with Abel and you.
One stands on the left hand, and one on the right,
Both bring equal measure of joy and delight.
Abel, you're wrong to say I love you more,
Make peace with your brother, and settle this score.

ABEL Brother, I'm sorry for what I just said,
If I say it again, may God strike me dead.

EVE That's better. Now, Cain, Abel's made his amends,
So no more sour looks. You two must be friends.
So come and joins hands like two loving brothers,
And when you've done that, give a kiss to your mother.

ABEL and CAIN grasp hands, then each gives EVE a kiss on the cheek.

Now I'm happy, and now I must leave you both here,
Your father's still poorly – he's near death, I fear.
Just as God said, he'll go back to dust
For the crime we committed in ages long past.
That sin's on our souls, that sin we all share,
The weight of our fate is a weight we must bear.

When our lives reach their end and our time comes around,
Our poor bones will lie deep under the ground.
But our souls may be saved, if we're honest and true
To the good Lord who made us, and give Him his due.
And so, for the fruits of the earth that you've raised,
Give all thanks to God, and sing out His praise.

EVE goes.

ABEL turns to CAIN.

ABEL Now brother, we must do as mother said
And offer up a sacrifice to God.

ABEL stands over the dead ram and speaks to GOD. As he does so, GOD enters, above.

Hear me, God, a simple man,
I tend my sheep as best I can
Among the hills, beneath the sun
Where grass grows rich and sweet.
This life you've made is good and fair
The earth, the sky, the sun, the air,
All pure joy, beyond compare,
A wonder and delight.

So I make sacrifice
To give thanks and make praise.
This fine, fattened sheep
From the flocks that I keep
Is my offering to you,
Your right and your due.

GOD This gift I'll receive
With blessing and grace,
And, as a sign, show
My benevolent face.

ABEL looks up.

ABEL A sudden glare,

A blaze of light,
My gift is good,
The day is bright.

CAIN now stands over his sheaf of wheat. When he speaks, he keeps his face lowered.

CAIN Hear my prayer, for here I stand.
I break the earth and dig the land,
And plough and plant with these two hands,
A true son of the soil.
But what with storm and flood and drought,
Sometimes my spirit near gives out –
My life's no thing to crow about,
Just drudge and sweat and toil.

So this that I bring
Is the least little thing,
A bundle of wheat
Laid here at my feet.
Take it or not,
It's all that you get.

GOD This gift I reject,
For it's made without grace.
To you, Cain, I show
The dark side of my face.

CAIN looks up.

CAIN The sky grows black,
The sun is hid,
A cold wind blows,
My gift's no good.

ABEL turns to CAIN.

ABEL Brother, this was not well done.

CAIN Brother, why don't you go home?
Get out my sight, leave me alone –

I want no words from you!

ABEL
You want to know why God's displeased,
And why it is your sacrifice
Was not accepted?

CAIN
Shut your face!
Or there's something I'll do
To shut it for you –

ABEL
Hear me, Cain.
I'll tell it to you straight and plain,
Your heart and soul are just too mean –

CAIN
And you're just too damn smart!
Abel-clever-arse, that's you!
God's favourite, and our mother's too!
You're really too good to be true!
Get lost! Sod off! Depart!

ABEL
Brother, I won't go from here
Till I've laid out plain and clear.
Your fault –

CAIN
I do not want to hear!

ABEL
You'll listen all the same!
To you this world that God has made
Is rotten, foul, and rank with weeds.
A loving heart is what you need.

CAIN
Shut up, in heaven's name!

ABEL
I speak the truth –

CAIN
Not one more word!

ABEL
Hear what I say.

CAIN
I think I've heard
Enough!

ABEL
Not yet –

CAIN
You little turd!
I'll silence you for good!

He strikes ABEL with the scythe as he speaks.

This blow will stop you going on!
And this! And this! And take this one
For luck! You'll wish, before I'm done,
You weren't our mother's favourite son!
I'll smash your skull! Break every bone!
What's that? Do I still hear you groan!
One more. And now you're good and gone!
And so I've done my deed.

ABEL lies on the floor. CAIN kneels beside him.

And there you lie
No light in your eye
You make no sound
Blood on the ground
No life, no breath
Why! This is death
That I have made.
A bloody deed –
A mystery –
Yet none shall see!
I'll dig a hole
And there your soul
Can lie well hid.
And so I'm rid
Of all my ills –
You'll lie there till
The crack of doom
Cold in your tomb –

This darksome deal of death has set me free,
And none shall know or guess that it was me.

He drags ABEL's body off.

EVE enters, sits, speaks to the audience.

EVE Well, he's dead. Passed from this world to the next. Not that it took much. One minute, there he was; the next, he wasn't. Gone. Like that. Not even a word. Didn't even bother to open his eyes. I'd just fetched him some water, on account of his mouth being so dry and so cracked. A little bowl of water. I dipped my fingers in it, and just dabbled them on his lips. Then I spoke his name. 'Adam?' I says to him. Then again. 'Adam.' Not that I expected him to say anything. I knowed he was too far gone for that. I just wanted him to know that I was there with him. And maybe that's what done it. Maybe he heard my voice and he knowed, and the knowing give him that final ease, and he let hisself go. For as I spoke his name that second time, and as I lifted my fingers away, his lips give a kind of flutter, and his breathing went all quick and shallow. And I felt it touch my hand – the faintest, softest breath – and then it stopped. And I waited for it to start up again, but it didn't. For him to take another breath, but he didn't. And then I knowed he'd never take another. I knowed he was gone. And perhaps that touch of his last breath to my hand was his way of saying goodbye to me. Perhaps. This death that God has give us is a bigger mystery, it seems to me, than life. I can't think no more about it. There's things to be done, but I can't do them yet. I'm too tired. I'll just lay down and have myself a little nap. Forty winks, and I'll be all right. Then I'll do what must be done.

She lies down and sleeps.

CAIN enters. He does not see her at first. There is a mark burned into his forehead.

CAIN It's done – he's down – but will he stay?
Will he ever give me rest?
No. My hands – stained with his blood –
My face – burned with this brand –
I thought the killing was the worst –
I thought when that was done it was all done –

Over and finished with –
But it seems it's just beginning –
Can the dead speak? Does blood have a voice?
His does…
I'd dug the hole, dug it deep,
I lifted him to lay him in the ground 23
When suddenly it seemed a voice cried out –

Offstage, we hear ABEL's voice.

ABEL Vengeance!

CAIN It cried out, loud and clear, and then again –

ABEL Justice!

CAIN I saw no one – there was no one there –
Only him, and he was cold,
His mouth it never moved,
But still that voice cried out –

ABEL Vengeance! Justice! Vengeance! 24

CAIN His blood, it was – his blood crying out!
His blood I spilled…
But still I took hold
And cast him down into the pit
And piled the earth and trod it down.

CAIN mimes treading the earth down on the grave. He speaks as if to the dead ABEL.

Now, brother, cry out if you can!
We'll see who's the better man!
You below, and me above – 25
And I'll have all our mother's love –
For you're deep down beneath the ground
Where your voice can make no sound –
And you never will be found.

Above, GOD speaks.

GOD Cain! Where is thy brother?

CAIN starts in fear.

CAIN A voice again? Who speaks now?

GOD Cain! Where is thy brother?

CAIN Not his! That's silenced now. Then whose?

GOD Cain! Where is thy brother?

CAIN Who speaks to me? Who calls me by my name?

GOD I speak to thee!
I call thee by thy name!
God, thy Lord and thy creator!

CAIN What dost thou want of me?

GOD Where is thy brother, Cain?

CAIN My brother? Abel, dost thou mean?

GOD Thou hast no other.

CAIN Wherefore should I know his whereabouts?
Do I tend him?
Am I my brother's keeper?

GOD Cain! What hast thou done?
Thy brother's blood cries out to me!
It howls and bellows from beneath the ground!
Thou hast slain him with thy hand!
Fall, Cain, thou killer!
Fall to thy knees thou murderer of men!

With a cry, as if knocked down, CAIN falls to his knees and clasps his hand to his face.

Cain, from this time you are cursed,
And into wilderness are cast,
There to wander till you breathe your last.

A fugitive and vagabond

Shall you walk in foreign lands,
Never to find home or peace again.

For this evil you have worked,
You shall dwell in outer-dark,
And here upon your face I set my mark!

And so my face is turned away from thee! 29
And nevermore shall thou, Cain, knowest me!

GOD turns and goes.

CAIN takes his face from his hands.

CAIN And this brand burned into my forehead sets me apart. By this I'm known as a murderer of men, a brother's killer, my crime proclaimed for all to see. So I must quit this place. Good riddance to it, then. It's been no boon to me. But where to go? God rises with the sun, so I'll head west. I've heard rumours of distant lands where people live, perhaps fashioned by some other God than mine. Or, better still, 30
owing allegiance to none. I'll try my luck there, set my feet westward, and bear this guilt and shame into the world.

He rises. As he's about to leave he sees EVE, sleeping.

Here's mother, sleeping. Let her rest. She'll wake soon enough to bitter knowledge. Two sons lost. But one at least can kiss her goodbye. *(He goes to kiss her, stops.)* I can't – my crime prevents me, holds me back. What kind of son is it can't kiss his own mother? No son at all. So now know I'm truly outcast and alone.

There's no more to be said. 31
I'm like one dead
To human love. And so
Without goodbye and fond farewell, I'll go.

CAIN goes. EVE stirs and wakes.

EVE Oh! I should never have had them forty winks. I feel so stiff… can hardly shift myself… I had a dream just now.

Strange it was. I was young again, and I'd give birth to a child. But such a child it was! A light shone from it, bright as a burning flame, and illuminating all the world around… and there was Adam young again and smiling, walking hand in hand with angels… and everything fresh and clear and new… and by the holy light that shone, I knew that we stood in Eden once again… all sins forgiven, all wrongdoing redeemed, all crimes pardoned and absolved… Then the light faded and I woke… and here I am – an old woman with aching bones and a dead husband – who's yet to be put in the ground. And where are my sons to help me? *(She calls out.)* Abel! Cain! Are you nearby? Cain! Abel! Come when your mother calls! Either they don't hear, or they don't want to. Well, I can't wait for them. Looks like I'll have to bury him meself. And hope my strength holds out. And pray that God will keep his soul in trust.

She stands.

Best get moving, when there's things to be done.
Death might strike among us, but life goes on.

She goes.

END OF THE THIRD PLAY

4 THE FLOOD

LUCIFER'S TRIUMPH

LUCIFER enters from Hell's mouth.

LUCIFER

I'm Lucifer, the Lord of Hell,
Come to greet you all, and tell
How in this world I have worked well
To win all souls to sin.
For time has passed and moved along,
The world now thrives and heaves and throngs
With folk, all speaking different tongues – ← Start soundscape. Gobbledeegook
You never heard such din!

But, whatever tongue they speak,
Their spirits are so frail and weak 1
They let me run amok, and wreak
My vengeance on them all. ← Fade out.
O, Joy! O! Rapture! O, such bliss!
There never were folk quite like this
For gross, indulgent wickedness –
I hold the world in thrall!

Pride and greed and treachery,
Murder and debauchery,
Wrath and lust and lechery –
These sins they know too well! 2
You hear me God? Hear what I say?
These folk are mine, and mine they'll stay!
Your time is past! You've had your day!
So – leave this world to hell!

As proof, now hear the evidence,
As these folk speak – and give offence.

The City of the Wicked

The chorus of the WICKED enter.

WICKED

And lo! we desired to build a great city,
a city the like of which the world had not yet seen,
that would be a wonder and a marvel to the eyes of men,
and for the building of which our name would be exalted.
And lo! and therefore was the city builded
with the strength of our hands and the desire of our hearts,
and we did dwell therein
and also therein we fashioned many forms of pleasure
which were for the ease and delight of our bodies,
for this was the City of Sensual Delight.
And lo! did we partake of each and every pleasure,
and of each and every pleasure did we drink deep.

Individuals now step forward and speak.

1 Amy

I desired my neighbour's wife,
And so I took my neighbour's life.
I killed my neighbour, killed him dead,
And so I took his wife to bed.

2 Sophie

There's nothing in this world so fair
As this mirror, in which I stare
To see my face, my eyes, my hair –
Beauty beyond all compare.
So I stand and stare…
Eyes, lips, skin, hair,
So rare, so fair.

3 Heather

My best friend grew a silver tree,
I asked my friend, 'Give it to me.'
'I can't, it's mine,' my friend did say –
But I took it anyway.

4 Elanor

Riddle-me-ree and riddle-me-roh,

What's the bestest place to go?
Down to the brothel, don't you know?
Where it's head-to-head and toe-to-toe.

All the chorus join in. 6

WICKED

Head-to-head,
Toe-to-toe,
That's the bestest, don't you know?
Fire me up
And watch me go,
Head-to-head
And toe-to-toe.

5 Stephanie

Here's a thing of pure delight,
To sleep all day and prowl all night.
Like a cat that creeps with the moon in its skull, 7
To prowl and stalk
Those few who walk
The midnight streets
On silent feet –
To prowl and stalk and pounce and spill
Their blood, and then to drink my fill.

6 Katherine

I had my table laid with meat,
And sat me down and I did eat,
And eat and eat and eat and eat,
And eat and eat and eat and eat. 8

All the chorus take this up.

WICKED

And eat and eat ← Sound Scape
And eat and eat Lard, Fat etc.
And eat and eat
And eat and eat!

7 Amy

I say to you, it makes no sense
To put this world behind a fence,
To hem it in with laws and rules…
All who hold to that are fools.

For here's the truth that we have found,
That Man was made to live unbound,
In unrestrained joy and delight,
Free to indulge his appetites!

All the chorus chant.

WICKED
All the day and all the night,
Indulge our human appetites!

Laugh

GOD'S RAGE

GOD enters above.

GOD
Wicked humankind! You vain and foolish
children of the earth! How far you've wandered
from my original intent, become
slaves to your own passions and desires! Hear
the voice of God, the one and only God
who first created you. You were my dream,
shimmering figures emerging out of
chaos, creatures of gold, forged in the flame
of this immense laboratory I call
creation. From base matter you were formed –
and to base matter you've returned, flung back
by flaws and cracks in your own natures. My
experiment has failed. I have no choice
but to destroy you, make a quick end, blast
you out of life, a single sudden bolt of
nuclear glare, power-packed for ultimate
destruction. I'll reduce you and this earth
to dust and ash, space-debris drifting through
creation's deep for all eternity.

LUCIFER
The game's won! Humankind is doomed!
The whole of space will be its tomb!
Stand back! Give me some elbow-room

While I strut and crow! 12
Their souls are mine! I'll get the lot,
And down in hell they'll writhe and rot,
For life down there is long and hot
And filled with pain and woe.

So I'll go now and wait
Down there by hell's gate
For the boom and the crash
Of God's nuclear blast –
Total annihilation
Of all his creation! 13
And amongst the ruins I will dance and sing
My triumph, and of all chaos be king!

LUCIFER exits into Hell's mouth.

CURTAIN

Flood Not Fire

GOD holds up a lightning-bolt, poised to strike.

GOD This deadly lightning-bolt is armed and primed.
One shot, and then it's done. The human race
will perish for its sins –

NOAH'S WIFE enters and speaks to God.

NOAH'S WIFE Now, just hold on!
What's all this about destroying the world? 14
Going to send the whole thing up in flames?
Blast it to pieces and then blast the pieces?
I never heard the like. That's a fine thing,
that is. Oh, yes, indeed. Very handsome
for the creator to destroy his own
creation. I have to say I'm taken
aback. I have to admit I'm gobsmacked!
Not that you haven't had provocation.

Gradually move 4ward.

Yes, I know this lot and their wicked ways,
And I know that they'll deserve everything
they've got coming. The world won't be sorry
to see the last of them! Oh, yes, you've got
justification, and you've got the right.
You made it, after all, and I suppose
you can destroy it. Yes, you've got the right,
but is it fair? Everything, I mean, all
that lives in the world, the very world itself,
to send it up in smoke? Now is that just?
Can you hear me, God? Are you listening?
Do you hear what I'm saying?

GOD Yes, I hear.

NOAH'S WIFE Good. I'm glad. I'm glad that you can hear me.
I'm only an old woman, and perhaps
I don't know much, but it appears to me
you're taking this whole thing a bit too far,
this plan of yours is just over the top.
Why should the blameless suffer for the crimes
of the guilty and wicked? If you can tell
me that and tell me true, I'll be content,
and go happy to my death.

GOD Blameless, you say?
Who's blameless in this world? You mean yourself?
Is that why you're here, to plead for your life?

NOAH'S WIFE Not just mine, but my husband's and my sons'.
I'm not saying we're perfect, not at all,
But we've always done our best to do
our best, live right and proper, and to keep
your ways.

GOD What is your husband's name?

NOAH'S WIFE Noah.
And there's our sons, Ham, Shem and Japheth,
and their three wives. We live out on our farm,

keeping beasts and raising crops and trying
to make a living as best we can.
And though it's not easy, we've not complained,
till now. And what I want to say is this –
it seems a pity and a shame that the likes
of us should perish for the likes of them,
that all the living creatures of this world –
yes, and the world itself – should be destroyed, 19
for I believe there is some good in it.
Let me say one thing more –

GOD You've said enough!
Enough to save your lives, and save the earth.
I'll temper my rage with mercy, send not
fire but flood, water to wash the world clean
of its wickedness. Go to your husband,
tell him he must build a boat.

NOAH'S WIFE A boat?
What kind of boat? 20

GOD One big enough to hold
Not only you and all your brood, but two
of every creature of the earth, one male
one female each.

NOAH'S WIFE What? Two of every kind?
That'll take some doing.

GOD It must be done.
Now go and start. Make haste. There's not much time.
In just one week the rains will tumble down,
The rivers rise, and all the world be drowned. 21

NOAH'S WIFE goes. GOD speaks to the audience.

God's spoken. Hear my words, you sinners all!
Your days are numbered, and hard rains shall fall!

THE WICKED MOCK AND JEER

The CHORUS OF WICKED now speak to each other. Lines are spoken individually.

WICKED Have you heard about Noah? He's building a boat!
What was that you said? Building a boat?
That's just what I said. He's building a boat.
A boat? What kind of boat?
A big boat. A very big boat.
A very big boat out there in the desert.
Why's he want to do that?
What's he building a boat for out in the desert?
What does he think? The sea's going to come to him?
He said God told him to.
God? God told him to build a boat?
God told him to build a boat in the desert.
Oh, well, that's all right, then, if God told him to.
I thought for a minute he might've gone mad.
But if God's told him to, he can't be, can he?
Completely sane, building a boat in the middle of the desert!

NOAH and NOAH'S WIFE enter, pushing a large boat. The WICKED jeer. NOAH and his WIFE work on the boat as the WICKED speak.

Here he is! Here's Noah and his boat!
Here's the man who's going to float
away on his boat –
The crazy old goat!

All laugh.

Here's his missis too! And all his family inside.
Hey, Noah! That's a fine boat you've built!
What are you going to do with it? Push it to the sea?
It's a long way, a very long way.
Tell you what, we'll save you the trouble.

We'll fetch you a bucket of water,
And you can float your boat on that!

Laughter again.

What did you build it for, Noah?
Come on, tell us, we're dying to know.
Who put that crazy idea in your head?
Was it God?
That's what somebody said.

NOAH Yes. It was God. God told my wife, and my wife told me.

WICKED His wife! It was his wife told him to build it!
He never even heard the word of God himself.
Hey, Noah! Did God tell your wife why you had to build it?
Did he give her any reason, any reason at all?
Or was it just a whim?
One of those divine fads for the bizarre and downright weird.
You know the kind of thing:
'Do thou this for me and thou shalt find favour in my sight
and be blessed among the multitude.'
Is it one of those tests of faith?
Like when he ordered Abraham to kill his own son?
Tell us, come on!
We're dying to know.

NOAH It's going to rain.

WICKED Eh? What's that?
What did you say?
I didn't quite catch it.
Say it again.

NOAH That's what he told her. It's going to rain. A heavy rain.
A hard rain. God's sending a rain to drown the world.

WICKED Did I hear him right?
Did he say what I just think he said?
It's going to rain.
God's going to flood the world.

God's going to drown us all.
Except for Noah.
Except for Noah and his family.

'For Noah is a just man, perfect in his generations, and he has found grace in the eyes of the Lord.'

As for the rest of us, we're doomed.
The corrupt and the wicked, we're going to die.
God's going to punish us all for our sins, and wash us clean off the face of the earth!

If he believes that, he'll believe anything!
What a dope!
What a sap!
What tripe!
What crap!
God's not going to send a flood
God's not going to drown the world
God's not going to do anything
Because there is no God, not anymore
Maybe there was once, but that was a long time ago
Before we got wise to the ways of the world
We've got other gods now, gods more suited to our tastes
Gods that don't give you a hard time
Gods who speak our language
Easy-going gods
Liberal-minded gods
If-it-feels-good-then-just-go-ahead-and-do-it kind of gods
And they're altogether much better than the old one
That wrathful, vengeance-taking God
Who was always too stubborn, too uncompromising
That God who just would never be satisfied
That God who you claim spoke to you and said he was going to drown the world.

As for that,
As for that hard, heavy rain that's going to fall –
It won't.

We've seen the long-range weather forecast
And the outlook's good
Clear skies, high-pressure, and non-stop sunshine.
So though we've said this before, we'll say it again,
One last time, just to make it plain,
There'll be no flood, 'cos there'll be no rain,
And, Noah, dear friend, you're completely insane!

NOAH'S WIFE
Ignore that lot. They've had their day. 32
God's flood will wash them all away.
He doesn't lie! His words are true!
Good riddance to the lot of you!

NOAH
Now, good wife, our work is done,
The boat's complete and everyone's
On board, and so it just remains
For us, before it starts to rain,
To shut ourselves within this ark –
Look there! The sky is growing dark!

NOAH'S WIFE
I see the clouds. I see them gather. 33
Looks like we're in for stormy weather.
Let's go and join our sons and daughters.
This land will soon be under water.

She goes into the boat.

NOAH
Now, I put my trust in God,
That he will save us from this flood.
And pray that when the storm is past,
The earth will be restored at last,
And life will be renewed again,
Washed clean of crime by holy rain. 34

NOAH goes into the boat.

The Great Deluge

GOD
Come storm and wrack!
Come lightning crack!
Let waters pour!
Let rivers roar
And rise to drown
The whole world round!
By power of God,
Come mighty flood!

WICKED
First there was a wind, a wind out of the west
And it brought dark clouds and heavy skies
And the clouds hung in rags, ripped by lightning
And the skies turned black, battered by thunder
Suddenly it was there, the storm all around us
Then the sky burst open
And the rains came

A crashing torrent
A blinding downpour
Tumbling
Hurtling
Sending us running
Back to our cities
Back to our homes
We locked the doors
We shuttered the windows
We crouched there, shivering, under our roofs
As the storm drummed and thundered about us
And we waited in fear for this terror to pass

But it didn't pass
It kept on coming
Things didn't get better
They just got worse

The rain just kept falling
The water kept rising
Rivers burst their banks
Became raging torrents
That flowed together
Churning and frothing
Flooding the fields
Drowning crops and cattle 38
And that huge tidal wave, that fury of water
Came crashing through the walls of the city
It ripped through our streets
It tore through our houses
It smashed its way in through the doors and windows
And nothing could withstand it
Nothing could resist it
Nothing could hold back that roaring frenzy
All was caught up and swept away
In the swell and the rush of that terrible onslaught 39

Nothing endured
None survived

The CHORUS OF WICKED now leave gradually, on their final lines.

And when at last it was over
When the rain stopped falling and the sky cleared
When the wind grew still and the waters settled
Our bodies floated and bobbed on the surface
The debris and wreckage of all humanity
For a short while they floated, a sorry flotsam,
Then sank, slowly, without trace or memory 40
Names and faces forgotten
Erased from the world's history
And our bones grew white in the dark's deep
And the sun shone clear on the silent waters.

All the chorus have gone.

THE BRIDGE OF LIGHT

NOAH'S WIFE looks out from the boat.

NOAH'S WIFE Noah, look! The rain's gone!
The storm's over and done!
And there shines the sun in the sky.

NOAH looks out.

NOAH Thank God for fresh air!
It's stifling in there!
All that dung everywhere – and it's high!

NOAH'S WIFE Don't fret about dung,
Take a breath, fill your lungs,
Soon you'll feel fit and strong, and much better.
Take a good look around –

NOAH Look at what? There's no land!
Not an inch of dry ground, only water!
And we're stuck on this boat –

NOAH'S WIFE Well, at least we're afloat
And without any doubt that's a blessing.

NOAH But for how long must we
Sail around on this sea?

NOAH'S WIFE Two months, maybe three – but that's guessing.

NOAH Three months? I can't wait
That long –

NOAH'S WIFE Listen, mate!
Don't get in a state, stop your crying!

NOAH But I'm sick, I feel ill!
I'm really not well!
Help me!

NOAH'S WIFE What's that smell?

NOAH Wife, I'm dying!

NOAH'S WIFE Shut up! Take a sniff
Of the air, there's a whiff
Of dry land, and if it proves right,
Soon we'll be home and dry –

NOAH Look up there! Oh, my!
It's a bridge in the sky made of light! 44

Pause.

Do you see it?

NOAH'S WIFE Oh, yes!
And, my love, it's my guess
That this wonder we see is a sign
From the Lord God above,
A sure mark of his love,
To tell us that everything's fine.

NOAH I feel better already,
My feet are quite steady – 45

NOAH'S WIFE Husband, get ready to cheer!
Over there I can see,
Rising out of the sea,
A hill and tree!

NOAH Come, let's steer
The boat over there,
Feel the wind in our hair,
Feel the glare and the heat of the sun!

NOAH'S WIFE We're all done with waiting,
The flood is abating,

NOAH Say goodbye to bad weather,

NOAH'S WIFE Soon we'll stand together,
Arm in arm –

NOAH Hand in hand

NOAH'S WIFE With our feet on dry land,

NOAH And the world good as new,

NOAH'S WIFE Made for me and for you,

NOAH Where we'll make a fresh life,

NOAH'S WIFE Dear husband – ← Look @ Katie

NOAH Dear wife,

NOAH'S WIFE Without care –

BOTH …for a new world's begun!

They push the boat offstage.

Music

God's Promise

As GOD speaks, angels unfold a rainbow across the stage.

GOD

Now earth's refreshed, and now the world's reborn,
A new sun rises, and new hopes are born.
This arc of shining, glistening light that curves
Above the world, above the sea and waves,
This bow of rainy colours in the sky
Is my avowal that no more will I
Destroy or devastate the human race –
From this time on I'll show more loving face.
And, though in ages still to come, these men
And women once more give themselves to sin,
Though Adam's first crime still corrupts their souls,
To win them back through love will be my goal.
And, to this end, I'll send to earth my son,
Divine made flesh and blood, the perfect man,
Who'll live and die, and rise again from death,
Defeating death and hell, and show the path
All humankind must take, from doom and fate,
To lead them once again through Eden's gates.
Let flood subside! Earth turn, shine stars and sun!
Let love pursue its course! Let time roll on!
For life's long road has hardly yet begun!

GOD goes.

End of the Fourth Play, and Part One

Part 2 Birth, Death and Resurrection

1 Mary

Four NEIGHBOURS enter.

NEIGHBOUR 1 You'll never guess what I've just heard!
It's juicy news! A little bird
Told me. You mustn't breathe a word!
It's just between us few.
You know young Mary –

NEIGHBOUR 2 The baker's daughter?

NEIGHBOUR 1 That's her. As pure as fresh spring water,
She reckons. Well, she's done what she shouldn't ought to.

NEIGHBOUR 2 Don't stop there!

NEIGHBOUR 3 Carry on!

NEIGHBOUR 4 Please do!

NEIGHBOUR 1 You know how la-di-dah she can be –

NEIGHBOUR 4 Too good for the likes of you and me.

NEIGHBOUR 1 She's not as pure as she makes out to be.
Quite the opposite.

NEIGHBOUR 2 Yes?

NEIGHBOUR 3 Tell us more!

NEIGHBOUR 1 I heard the news just the other day.
It seems she's let herself get led astray.

NEIGHBOUR 2 You mean…?

NEIGHBOUR 1 Yes! She's in the family way!

NEIGHBOUR 3 She's not!

NEIGHBOUR 1 She is!

NEIGHBOUR 2 No!

NEIGHBOUR 4 Are you sure?

NEIGHBOUR 1 It's God's honest truth! I know for a fact
That her maidenhead's no longer intact,
And she's got a bundle stuffed in her sack!

NEIGHBOUR 2 How awful!

NEIGHBOUR 3 Poor girl!

NEIGHBOUR 4 What a plight!

NEIGHBOUR 2 I'll go right to the foot of our stairs!

NEIGHBOUR 3 To think such a thing could happen to her!

NEIGHBOUR 4 I'm not surprised. She had too many airs
And graces. It just serves her right!

NEIGHBOUR 2 What a scandal! How've her folks taken the story?

NEIGHBOUR 1 Her old man's gone mad! He's raging like fury,
And all set to kick out his precious young Mary.

NEIGHBOUR 2 And her once his pride and joy.

NEIGHBOUR 3 And that young man of hers? What does he say?

NEIGHBOUR 1 I don't know. He's been working away,
But I've heard that he's due back today,
So I reckon we'll see feathers fly.

NEIGHBOUR 4 I think it's disgusting! A thorough disgrace!
If I was her I wouldn't dare show my face
In public. I wouldn't be in her place
For all the gold in the ground.
Young people today, they think they can flout
All the laws of convention –

NEIGHBOUR 2 What was that shout?

NEIGHBOUR 3 Her fiancé! He's back! He must've found out!

NEIGHBOUR 2 It's amazing how word gets around.

NEIGHBOUR 1 Don't say a word
About all you've heard.
Play wide-eyed and dumb,
And we'll have some real fun!

JOSEPH enters.

JOSEPH Where is she? Where's that woman of mine?
Where's the wench that I'm bound to wed?
I've looked everywhere,
But can't find hide nor hair,
And there's something between us that needs to be said.

To NEIGHBOURS.

Have you seen her?

NEIGHBOUR 1 Who?

JOSEPH Mary, my intended.

NEIGHBOUR 2 Have we seen her?

JOSEPH Yes! Have you?

NEIGHBOUR 3 No.

NEIGHBOUR 4 Is it urgent?

JOSEPH I'll say!
The news I've heard today
Has come like a thunderbolt out of the blue.

NEIGHBOUR 2 Sounds like it's not good.

JOSEPH It's not. It's the worst
A chap in my position could hear.
My wife that's to be
Has been cheating on me.

NEIGHBOUR 3 You mean, she's been unfaithful?

JOSEPH Yes, that's what I fear. 8

NEIGHBOUR 4 What, Mary? That innocent, blameless young lamb?
That sweet young virgin girl has been caught?
Why, everyone knows
She's as pure as the snow!

JOSEPH Up to this minute, that's just what I thought!

NEIGHBOUR 1 Who told you? Who's been telling this tale?

JOSEPH Who hasn't? It's news all over the place.
She's been off with some bloke,
They said. Ain't it a joke?
Some of them even laughed right in my face! 9

NEIGHBOUR 2 So people are saying your Mary's been fooling
Around with some feller? Did they tell you no more?

JOSEPH They certainly did!
She's having a kid!
And I'm not the father, I know that for sure!

NEIGHBOUR 3 Well! I never did! Did you?

NEIGHBOUR 4 No, I never!
The gossip some folks spread –

NEIGHBOUR 1 Let's not jump the gun.
How's he know it's the truth? 10
What he wants is some proof.

NEIGHBOUR 4 He'll get that right now.

JOSEPH What?

NEIGHBOUR 4 Here comes her old man.

MARY'S FATHER enters and speaks to JOSEPH.

MARY'S FATHER Don't say nothing! Don't speak a word!
I can see by the look on your face that you've heard
How that wretched, no-good daughter of mine's
Brought me shame.

JOSEPH It's true, then?

MARY'S FATHER Mate, she's three months gone!

JOSEPH I just can't believe it!

MARY'S FATHER You better had!
It's only too clear she's no longer a maid.

JOSEPH But how did it happen?

MARY'S FATHER The usual way
A girl gets herself in the family way.

JOSEPH She's gone and betrayed me!

MARY'S FATHER Don't snivel and moan!
Set your jaw! Stand up straight, and act like a man!
You can't let her make a fool out of you!

JOSEPH She's already done that, so, what can I do?

MARY'S FATHER Let her see that you won't take this thing lying down!
A bloke's got to show he won't be pushed around.
'Cos women are wicked, that's what I believe.
There's none of them good, all the way back to Eve.
They flutter their lashes, put paint on their faces,
Come acting the innocent, all airs and graces.
But don't be deceived by their tricks and their lies,
They're nothing but devils got up in disguise.
Mother and sister, daughter and wife,
They're all of them born to bring us to grief.
They're liars, deceivers, harlots and whores,
Rotten, the lot of them, down to the core.
So I give you permission, as her dear old dad,
To give her the biggest beating she's had.
And when you've done that, cast her out of your sight,
Both her and her kid, you'll be doing what's right.
We'll show these here females we're wise to their games –

MARY and her MOTHER have entered.

MARY'S MOTHER Husband! Your words ought to make you ashamed!
Can you hear what you're saying? What rubbish you spout!
This here's your own daughter you're talking about!

MARY'S FATHER She's no child of mine!

MARY'S MOTHER That's enough of that! How
Can you speak such hard words when she's standing here now?
Look her straight in the face, then call her a whore!
Go on! Tell her she's not your child anymore!
You can't, can you? No! You don't have the gall!
Your mouth might be big, but your mind's mean and small! 15

To JOSEPH.

As for you, letting this old fool lead you astray,
When you've not heard a word of what she's got to say,
Where's the love that you vowed? Where's the faith and the trust?
The first hint of trouble, and they're gone with the dust!
But that's men all over, it's only their pride
They care about. Both of you turn my insides!

JOSEPH I've been wronged!

MARY'S MOTHER Have you? Really? How would you know that? 16

JOSEPH Is she pregnant?

MARY'S MOTHER Well, yes, she is, I admit –

MARY'S FATHER There's no more to be said!

MARY'S MOTHER That's enough out of you!
What's going on here is between just these two.
And it's not all been said, there's a whole lot more.
Let her speak. Hear her out. You know that it's fair.

JOSEPH All right, I'll listen, I'll hear her side
Of the story. And after that I'll decide
If I've been wronged or not. 17

MARY'S MOTHER Come on, love, speak clear.
Tell him what you told me. There's nothing to fear.

MARY I'll try to tell you what happened,
how it came about that I'm having this child.
I don't know if you'll understand it.
I'm not sure I understand it myself,
nor if I can tell it right.
But, anyway, I'll do my best.

It was about three months ago, the beginning of spring,
I went into the hills just outside the town.
It's quiet there, peaceful, the air's clean and fresh,
and there are some flowers growing there,
little blue and white flowers
that I've never seen growing anywhere else.
I wanted to pick some and take them home,
to put in a jar on the windowsill.
It was a warm day, the sun was shining, the sky was clear,
and after I'd picked the flowers I sat down on the grass,
just to rest for a few minutes.
So warm and still, it was,
one of those days when everything seems to slow down,
and it feels like it might last forever.
So I lay back and looked up at the sky,
and it was so blue and deep and far away,
and the sun was so warm on my face,
and I could hear the birds singing and insects humming…
My eyes closed, I stretched my arms,
and I began to fall asleep…

Then suddenly it all changed,
suddenly I was awake and everything was different,
sharper and clearer, somehow.
The grass was trembling,
the whole hill kind of rippling as if it were alive.
And the sky wasn't far away anymore,
it was pressed up close against my face,
and all around me there was this light,

a shower of golden light falling,
and getting brighter and brighter,
as if the sun itself was coming down to earth,
and I could hear a kind of singing, 21
a singing coming from deep down somewhere,
a singing that ran through my whole body,
and all the time the light was growing stronger,
until there was nothing but that light and I was part of it.

And then it was gone, and everything was ordinary again.
I was lying on the grass with my eyes open.
The sky, the hill, the sun, ordinary, just like they'd been before,
and it was just an ordinary day.
So I stood up, I picked up the flowers I'd gathered,
I went back down the hill, I came home, 22
and put the flowers in a jar on the windowsill,
and I didn't say anything to anybody about what had happened,
because I wasn't sure what had happened,
or if it had really happened at all.
But now I know it did.
Now I know what it was.
Because I'm having this child,
and I don't really know how to explain it to you,
except to say that somehow that day
the hill and the sky and the flowers and the sun 23
became this life that's growing inside me,
and I don't know what it means or why,
but I'm not ashamed.
I know I have nothing to be ashamed of.
This life is something sacred and special,
something pure, something holy,
and it makes me want to laugh and cry out, to shout and dance,
I want to stamp my feet hard on the ground,
and raise my face to the sky,
and sing some song of joy and praise… 24

That's my story, that's what happened,
and I don't know if you'll believe me or not.

I won't blame you if you don't.
All I can tell you is the truth.
That's all there is. I've nothing more to say.

MARY'S FATHER Well! That takes the biscuit! Do you really expect
We'll believe all this claptrap? You'll be telling us next
That God's the father of this here child!
I've never heard nothing so daft or so wild!

MARY It's the truth –

MARY'S FATHER Stop your lying!

MARY I'm not –

MARY'S FATHER Just take care,
Or you'll feel the back of my hand –

MARY'S MOTHER Don't you dare
Raise your fist to our daughter! If you even try
You'll be dealing with me! Then we'll see feathers fly!

MARY'S FATHER But she's saying that she got this baby of hers
From a few rays of sunshine and a bunch of wild flowers!
And if you're telling me that you think she's not lying,
Then I'm telling you that you need certifying!

MARY'S MOTHER Will you give it a rest? No more of your noise!
We've all heard enough of the sound of your voice!
If all you can do is bluster and shout,
Then it's best you say nothing, and keep your trap shut!

Joseph, you've heard her, and you know her well.
Do you really think that she'd spin you a tale
So fantastic as this one, if she wasn't sure
It was true? Has she ever lied to you before?

JOSEPH No, she hasn't.

MARY'S MOTHER So why should she be lying now?

JOSEPH I'd like to believe her, but I don't see how
Such a tale could be true.

MARY'S MOTHER Why shouldn't it be?
This world's full of wonders, if we'd eyes to see,
And minds that were open, and hearts that were pure –
There's miracles happening outside our front doors!
And there's more to this life than meets anyone's eye,
And though believing's not easy, I think we must try.
'Cos even though opening our hearts might bring pain,
If we keep them closed, we lose more than we gain.

JOSEPH speaks to MARY.

JOSEPH You know I'm a simple chap, perhaps not too bright,
And the truth of your tale I can't tell aright,
And up to this minute I was set to believe
That you'd played me false, and I'd been deceived.
I was fixing to tell you that our vows were ended,
'Cos you'd broken our promise, and it couldn't be mended,
That I'd side with the town in casting you out –
But now all those words are stuck in my throat.
'Cos there's something about the tone of your voice
And the look in your eyes that leaves me no choice
But to say I'll believe every word of your tale,
Though there's some here, I know, who'd call me a fool.
And if that's the case, then fool let me be,
I'd rather be that than in their company.
Let others cry out you've committed a sin,
I won't, I'll stand by you, through thick and through thin.
And though what's taken place I don't understand,
I'll take it on trust, and give you my hand,
And be proud to call you my partner and wife,
And pledge you my love for the rest of my life.

MARY'S MOTHER Good on you, Joe! Spoken like a true man!
It makes me proud to have you for a son.
If all men could show loving kindness like yours,
We'd have much less trouble in this poor world of ours.

MARY'S FATHER But –

MARY'S MOTHER Husband, before you speak, just take a pause,
You've caused enough trouble with that tongue of yours.
Don't go stirring up more, just come along home.
We've outstayed our welcome. It's time we were gone.

MOTHER and FATHER go.

JOSEPH As for us, I think we'd best pack up and leave this place,
And try to find some other town
Where folks' hearts aren't so full of scorn
And hate, and your child can be born
And live its life in peace.

MARY and JOSEPH go.

NEIGHBOUR 1 Well! What do you make of all that?

NEIGHBOUR 2 I'm amazed!

NEIGHBOUR 3 I'm speechless! I'm gobsmacked!

NEIGHBOUR 4 I'm not surprised.
I knew that she'd pull the wool over his eyes,
I mean, he was never too bright.

NEIGHBOUR 1 It'll all end in tears.

NEIGHBOUR 2 Do you think so?

NEIGHBOUR 1 It's plain
That child of hers won't bring them nothing but pain,
And misery and grief, and their hearts will be torn,
And they'll both rue the day that it ever was born.
You mark my words. See if I'm right.

NEIGHBOURS go. CURTAIN

END OF THE FIFTH PLAY

2 The Shepherds

MOSES enters.

MOSES
Oh, by heck! It's cold! Brass-monkey weather
without a doubt! My feet are well-nigh froze!
My nose is numb, my fingers have no ends.
I wouldn't be surprised if they dropped off.
What a God-forsaken, unholy night
to be keeping watch out here in the hills!
Who'd be a shepherd on a night like this?
Not me if I could help it, but I can't.
Born to it, I was, just as my poor dad
was before me, and all our wretched kind,
all the way back to Adam, damn his eyes!
For his crime all men stand condemned, and none
so worse as we who walk these hills alone.
They say hell's hot, and burns damned souls in flames
of endless torment. But I say it's not!
I say that there's no torment greater than
this ice that freezes flesh to solid bone,
and petrifies all living things to stone.
See how the world lies white, as drained of life,
all ghostly pale beneath midwinter's moon!
On nights like this they say that spirits walk,
foul ghosts and goblins, all the brood of hell
set free to stomp the earth. And on a night
like this one I could well believe it's true.
It fair gives me the shivers, I admit –
I ain't ashamed to say that I'm fair frit!

ISAAC calls from offstage.

ISAAC
Hallo!

MOSES
Eh, up! What's that?

ISAAC Who's there?

MOSES Hallo?

ISAAC Hallo yourself!

MOSES Who is it?

ISAAC Is that you?

MOSES It might be! Who's that there?

ISAAC It's only me!

MOSES Who're you?

Offstage, ABRAM calls.

ABRAM Who is it?

ISAAC Moses.

MOSES Eh?

ISAAC What?

ABRAM Who?

ISAAC Moses, I said!

MOSES You can't be?

ABRAM Who said that?

MOSES I did!

ABRAM Who did?

ISAAC He did.

MOSES Who's that?

ISAAC Isaac.

MOSES But he ain't here!

ISAAC I know I ain't! I'm here!

ISAAC enters.

MOSES Isaac! It's you!

ISAAC I know. At least, I did
Until just then, but now I'm not so sure.

ABRAM enters, carrying a box.

ABRAM Isaac! There you are. And Moses!

MOSES Abram!
Thank God you ain't a ghost.

ABRAM I feel like one.
So cold I am right through I might be dead.

MOSES You ain't alone.

ISAAC Here, have a nip of this.

Takes out a bottle.

MOSES What is it, Isaac?

ISAAC My own concoction.
It's guaranteed to stoke your poor soul's flame,
and bring some life back both to breath and blood.

MOSES Let's try some then. *(Drinks.)* By heck, it don't taste bad!
It warms you sure enough. I'll have some more –

ISAAC Not too much, now –

MOSES It gets right to the root,
and like a dog knows where to bite –

ISAAC A nip
was all I said! Have any more and you'll
soon feel its teeth dug deep in where it hurts.

MOSES One more before I'm done. Good God above!
But that's some prize brew you've got bottled there.

ABRAM Can I have some?

MOSES Here, Abram, take a swig.

This stuff of Isaac's will set fire your soul.
Drink, and I vouch you'll no more feel the cold.

ABRAM drinks.

ABRAM That's good, that is. That's good. That's very good.
Oh, yes, it's very good. It's really good –

MOSES I think he likes it, Isaac.

ISAAC There's no doubt
He thinks it's good.

ABRAM It is! It's very good!
My lambkin would like this.

MOSES What's that you said?

ISAAC Your lambkin?

ABRAM Yes, I've got it in this box.

ISAAC You've got a lamb in there?

ABRAM I have.

ISAAC What for?

ABRAM He was born this night, an hour ago,
I found him in the snow, his mother dead,
and bleating all his sorrows to the world.
Poor little orphan mite, it touched my heart,
to hear his pitiful cries, and so I
picked him straight up and put him in this box,
with straw to keep him warm, but what he needs
is sustenance to give him strength and heart.
And that there drink –

ISAAC Now, Abram, say no more.
For no lambkin was this concoction brewed!
It's got the devil in it, all the flames
and fires of fearsome hell concealed within
its liquid. This ain't no drink for lambkins!
One sip of that would blow his head right off.

MAK enters.

MAK Sounds like the drink for me, then. Give it here,
I'll drink hell's torment down and spew it up
within the hour.

MOSES Mak! What you doing here?

MAK Nothing much. Just out for a stroll.

MOSES A stroll
on such a night as this? You must be mad!
Unless you're up to something –

MAK Up to what?
What would I be up to? Tell me that!

ISAAC What wouldn't you? There ain't no scheming trick
nor underhand, conniving enterprise

but you ain't got your finger stuck in it.
A low-down, no-good scoundrel's what you are,
A villain through and through, and I for one
wouldn't trust you as far as I could spit!

MAK I take it that's a no to the drink, then.

ISAAC You take it right. I've made my feelings plain.

MAK You have indeed. But what about these two?
Moses? Abram? How do you regard me?
Friend or foe? Come on, speak up.

MOSES A rogue
You was born, Mak, and rogue you'll always be.
There's no denying it.

ABRAM I say the same.
For thieving, one like you I've never known.
You'd steal milk from a baby's bottle.

MAK Me?
Now would I do a thing like that?

ABRAM You did!
Last time you was round our house you done
That very thing, and left our little one
crying for his supper.

MAK I was thirsty!

ISAAC You're a thief! And a liar! And a cheat!
And I think that I'm speaking for us all
when I say your company's not wanted.
You're up to no good, if I'm not mistook,
so make scarce of yourself, and sling your hook!

MAK Hard words, these are, from them as I regard
my dearest friends, but I'll not take offence.
I'm not a one to hold a grudge, and so,
to prove this to you, I'll give you the news
I came to bring you.

MOSES What news might that be?

MAK It's this. An evil spirit walks abroad
the hills tonight, and has been seen within
the hour.

ABRAM An evil spirit, did you say?

MAK I did, and say again, a fearful ghost
haunts the world this night.

MOSES What kind of ghost?

MAK One most terrifying to behold,
with staring eyes, and fearful horrid looks,
and horns upon its head, and long sharp claws
for ripping out a person's innards! Aye,
and makes a horrid, howling noise, like this –

He howls. The three jump.

ABRAM That is a fearsome sound.

MAK I know it is,
and more so when made by the thing itself
than my pale imitation.

ISAAC How'd you know
this demon makes that noise, and how it looks?

MAK With these two eyes I saw it, with these ears
I heard that sound, but kept my courage up,
and cried 'Aroint thee, ghost, and get thee gone!'
and stuck two fingers out like this, and straight
the spirit vanished – but will come again,
I'm sure of it. And so directly I
came to warn you of this apparition,
as would any friend. And, having done so,
I'll bid you goodnight.

MAK goes. CURTAIN

ABRAM Mak, wait…!

ISAAC Let him go.
We're all well shut of him, and his daft tales.

ABRAM You think they're daft?

ISAAC I do.

MOSES I ain't so sure,
for as I waited here for you, alone,
I felt a chilling to my blood, the hair
upon my head did stand, my very soul
did freeze and shiver, as some hellish ghoul
had passed close by.

ISAAC Moses, you surprise me!
I never took you for the nervous kind,
nor one to take note of superstition!
The winter's cold did freeze your blood and flesh,
and make your hair stand straight, no more than that!
I don't believe in imps or ghouls or ghosts,
nor no other supernatural kin.
There's nought but God-made walks this earth –

Offstage, a howl.

ABRAM What's that?
You hear it?

ISAAC Yes –

MOSES Ssh!

The howl again.

ABRAM There it is again!
And getting closer!

MOSES Aye, I think it is!

ISAAC It's just a wolf.

MOSES No wolf makes noise like that.

ABRAM Nor nothing mortal!

The howl again. 22

MOSES Now it's closer still!

ABRAM It's almost here!

MOSES Time, then, that we was gone!

ABRAM I'm with you there.

MOSES You ready?

ABRAM Yes.

MOSES Let's run!

ABRAM and MOSES run off, leaving the box behind. ISAAC calls after them.

ISAAC Moses! Abram! What d'you think you're doing? 23
Where are you? Come back here! There ain't no ghosts!
Are we cowards to be afraid of sounds
And noises in the night? Let's stand like men
and face whatever comes!

The howl again, close.

On second thoughts
I think you might be right!

ISAAC runs off.

MAK enters, laughing.

MAK You see them go? 24
Running as if old Lucifer himself
was at their heels. And so he was, of sorts,
'cos Mak's the biggest devil ever walked
this mortal earth, and greater wickedness
no living man has ever worked than me.
And though it's not their souls I'm after, yet
I'll take a little something for my gain.
Now what's this here they've got inside this box?
Well, now, fancy that! A little lambkin!

Poor creature! Did they leave you all alone?
Abandon you, did they, out in the cold?
You're an orphan, now, a motherless child,
You'd best come home with me. Oh, look! See how
you're shivering! As soon as we get home
I'll stoke a fire to warm you to your bones.
Before you know it, you'll be roasting hot!
And then, to celebrate, we'll have a feast,
and you'll be the chief guest – and the main dish!

MAK goes with the box.

ABRAM, MOSES and ISAAC enter.

ABRAM Has the spirit gone?

MOSES I think it has. Look,
see here, its tracks set in the snow.

ISAAC No ghost
made them. They're mortal-made, of flesh and blood.
We've been played false, my lads, and made fools of!
If I ain't wrong – and I'm sure that I'm not –
That ghost we heard was none other than Mak.

ABRAM You mean, he's dead?

ISAAC He ain't, but you are, Abram!
Dead from the neck up!

MOSES Do you mean that Mak
made all that noise and scared us off?

ISAAC I do.

MOSES But what had he to gain from that?

ISAAC His lamb.

ABRAM My little lambkin?

ISAAC Yes, that's right. It's gone.

ABRAM Mak's stole him! That rotten, thieving villain!

We've got to get him back!

ISAAC And so we will.
Straight off we'll make our way round to Mak's house
and pay him back full sore for this foul crime.

MOSES And if we're quick, we'll catch him just in time!

ABRAM To hang his insides on the washing-line!

ABRAM, MOSES and ISAAC go.

MAK and SAL enter, MAK with the box.

SAL Mak, my love, but you are a man and half,
a wonder-worker, sure. You make me proud
to be your wedded wife. Come here to me
and let your dearest Sal give you a kiss.

She kisses him and hugs him.

How I love the taste of stale tobacco
on your breath, and the smell of your strong sweat
is sweeter to me than some posh perfume.
Let other wives proclaim their men's virtues!
I'll sing the praises of your vices, and
curse Lucifer that he didn't make more.

MAK Loose me, Sal! Your loving will crack my ribs!
I'm fit to bust! I'll die for lack of breath!

She looses him.

That's better. Now. Just take this gift I've brought,
and never more let it be said that when
Mak comes home, he comes home empty-handed.

SAL Such a fine gift it is as well, a lamb,
all succulent and sweet, all fleshy firm,
just like a baby lying in its cot!
I can almost taste it now, that roast meat
sizzling on the spit, the hot fat dripping
in the flames and running down our chins!

MAK And tasting better all for being stole.

SAL Why, so it will! Let's get it stuck and bled,
let's skin and gut it, and prepare our feast!

MAK Here's my knife, newly-sharpened with a point
to pierce the wind. I'll do the job right now.
Cut its throat and then it's done –

SAL Hold on!

MAK What's up?

SAL Not yet!

MAK Why not?

SAL Hang on a bit!
I heard a noise.

MAK What noise?

SAL Somebody's there,
outside the door.

MAK Who?

SAL Three chaps wearing caps.

MAK It's them!

SAL Who?

MAK The ones I pinched the lamb off!
I thought I'd fooled them!

SAL Seems like you were wrong!
They're knocking at the door!

MAK I can hear them!
The noise they make'd wake the wretched dead!

SAL Don't keep them waiting, let them in.

MAK You what?
Sal, have you lost your mind? They'll murder me!
String me up for thieving!

SAL No, they won't. 34
From what you've said they ain't possessed of brains.

MAK They don't have one between them.

SAL Well, that's it.
You and me, we'll run circles around them.
Now let them in. I'll be back in a bit.
Just keep them talking, and be of good cheer,
I'll save your skin, sweet husband, never fear.

SAL goes, with the box. MAK goes to another side of the stage, mimes opening the door, and MOSES, ISAAC and ABRAM enter.

MAK Come on, good mates! Well-met! You must be froze! 35
Don't stand out there, come in, and warm yourselves
before our fire. It's blazing in the hearth.

ISAAC Mak –

MAK Now, I know what you're going to say.
You've come to apologise for saying
those nasty things about me. There's no need!
I told you I'm not one to take offence.

MOSES Now, listen, Mak –

MAK Did that spirit show up?
The one I told you of? 36

MOSES Something showed up,
a nasty piece of work it was, all right,
a devil through and through, and double-damned
for making off with our poor Abram's lamb.

MAK That goblin stole your lamb? Well, I'll be blowed!

ABRAM It weren't no goblin, Mak, as well you know!

MAK What do you mean?

ISAAC He means that you're the thief
that took his lamb!

MAK Are you accusing me
Of stealing?

MOSES Yes, we are!

MAK I'm really hurt!
How could you think that I'd do such a thing?

ISAAC We don't think it, Mak, we know it, and
we've come to take that lamb – and have revenge!

SAL enters, carrying the lamb wrapped in a blanket.

SAL What's going on? What's all this row about?
Hush up your noise! You'll wake my baby up!

MOSES Your baby, did you say?

SAL That's right, I did.
He's sleeping peaceful as a little lamb,
and I don't want him waking with your noise.
So keep it quiet!

ISAAC Well, now, there's a surprise!
I never knew you had a baby, Mak.

MAK Neither did I –

SAL Till he came home just now.
I kept it secret from him.

MAK Yes, she did!
A right surprise, it was, when I walked in
and saw that baby there.

ABRAM It must've been!
Let's have a look at him –

SAL I'd rather not.
The little chap's just now got off to sleep.

MOSES Only a peek.

ISAAC A little look.

ABRAM Go on.

MOSES We promise not to wake him. 40

SAL Well, all right.
But just one peep each.

ISAAC That's all that we want.

SAL Here you are, then. Take a look.

ISAAC My God!
He's hairy, ain't he? Look at all them curls!
And them great ears! I never saw such ears
stuck on a baby's head!

MOSES Let me see. Mak!
This baby here's your spitting image! See, 41
there in the middle of his face, that nose!
Only your kid could have a nose that size!

SAL That's enough! You'll wake him up!

ISAAC Hang on,
there's Abram yet to see him. Come on, mate,
and take yourself a good look at this babe.
Well, Abram, what you think?

ABRAM That there's a lamb!

MAK He is, I know, just like a little lamb –

ABRAM I don't mean 'like', I mean that's what he is! 42
A little lambkin, not a child at all!
And not just any lamb –

SAL Oh, no! My child!
Some devil's come and stole my child away,
and left me this here changeling in its place!
O mercy me! O woe! Alas!

ISAAC Shut up!
If there's been any stealing going on,

it ain't no devil's work, but yours and Mak's!

MOSES That's right! That's Abram's lamb you've got in there,
and if we hadn't come in time, no doubt
you'd both be feasting on the creature's flesh!

ABRAM You rogue! You thief! You villain!

MAK Listen lads,
let me explain –

ISAAC We'll hear no words from you!
You've been found out, tried, judged, and now condemned,
all that remains is sentence to be passed.

They take hold of MAK.

MOSES Take him outside and tie him to a tree,
then beat him black and blue, leave not a bone
unbroke, and stick a crown upon his head
and call him King of Thieves, so all the town
will know him for the mean-hearted, low-down
villain that he is!

SAL Oh, sirs, have mercy
on my man! I beg you, please, have pity!

ISAAC There ain't no pity due to his kind, no,
nor mercy neither. Our hearts are closed tight.
Out with him! Tie him up!

ABRAM And let me be
the one to cast the first blow –

An ANGEL appears, above.

ANGEL Halt! Hold your hands!

MOSES Who said that? Was it you?

ISAAC It weren't.

ABRAM Nor me.

MOSES Somebody spoke.

ANGEL They did! Look up and see!

They look up and see the angel. 46

ABRAM A ghost!

MOSES Help!

ISAAC Run!

SAL Oh, mercy!

MAK Me first!

ANGEL Stop!
You foolish mortals! Open up your eyes!
I'm no ghost, but an Angel of the Lord,
a messenger from heaven, sent to bring
good news to you, and turn your hearts from wrath 47
to mercy, and so it is my command
you all should grip your hands in brothers' love,
forgive all faults, embrace, and each to each
swear true friendship.

ISAAC To him? We can't do that!

MOSES This man's a thief, deserving of our wrath!

ABRAM We've vengeance sworn, and vengeance we will take!

ISAAC Show love to Mak? No! Never!

ANGEL But you must!
If not, your lives are worth no more than dust! 48
I tell you, there's a new day coming soon,
and when it does, you'll see a brighter sun
shine in the sky than ever yet has shone.
And those whose hearts are fortified with love
shall bathe forever in sustaining warmth,
their souls shall join with it, all shall be one.
But if your hearts are bound with bands of hate,

they'll be unable to endure the heat
that shines from such a sun, and so will scorch
and wither at their roots, and so be lost
from life and love and joy for evermore.

And as a sign of this new-coming dawn,
down in the town a baby has been born,
God's only son, who'll rid the world of sin,
you'll find him in a stable, by an inn.
Go there now, and gaze upon the face
of this child, born to bring the world to grace,
and kneel before him with pure minds and hearts.
Embrace, forgive each other – and depart.

ISAAC Let's go without delay and seek this child,
for even now I feel a change of heart.

MOSES And so do I. Mak, take my hand.

ABRAM And mine.
We'll no more be your enemies.

MAK Good friends,
I take your love, and give you mine, and swear
that from this time on I shall be reformed.

SAL So all our hearts are turned and changed about,
Our lives re-made anew. Now let us go
and kneel before this child, whose birth has brought
such sudden transformation to our hearts.

The three SHEPHERDS, MAK and SAL go. The ANGEL speaks to the audience.

ANGEL The drama that you've seen enacted here
has been but shadow of the true event –
for all that happens in human affairs
is but reflection of the divine, seen
in a darkened mirror. And so the lives
of every man and woman on this earth,
now and to come, have being in the birth

of God's son, whose coming I foretold.
That being done, and my purpose achieved,
I'll melt now into insubstantial air,
less than a breath, and leave this platform bare.

The ANGEL goes.

END OF THE SIXTH PLAY

3 THE SLAUGHTER OF THE INNOCENTS

JOSEPH enters and speaks to the audience.

JOSEPH

Last night I had this dream.
I'd woken from sleep, it seemed,
in the very dark of night,
but outside, some deep red light
was glowing and flickering, and strange sounds
were coming from all around. → START soundscapes 'Joseph, Beware etc.'
I stood, went to the door
and looked outside, and there I saw
a terrible sight.
Men filled the street,
and they were herding animals of every kind
into a pen, where others, with clubs in hand,
were butchering them where they stood,
and their arms and their hands were thick with blood.
Those animals not yet killed struggled and pushed
in a seething crush
of terror, trying to escape,
but there was no hope.
The men with twisted faces laughed and grinned,
while all about them the howling din
of the slaughtered animals rose,
and my heart froze
to hear that dreadful song,
for the creatures all cried out with human tongues.

I woke then, with sweat on my face, ← → STOP!
and I knew that we had to leave this place,
go now, straightaway,
before the break of day,
like fugitives, take to the road and flee
far from this country.

Where will it lead? I don't care,
as long as it's away from here,
for the bitter taste of fear in my mouth
tells me this town is a place of death.

JOSEPH goes.

KING HEROD enters and speaks to the audience.

HEROD

I am Herod, this country's king,
I wear the whole land like a ring
upon my finger, shining bright,
I like to keep it close and tight,
it fits me like a well-made suit,
for I'm a monarch absolute!
Every village, farm and town
belongs to me, they're mine alone.
My word's the law, without my say
the sun won't rise at break of day,
I'm Lord of All, Herod the Great!
When I fart folks sit up straight!

But now I've heard a prophecy
that's really put the wind up me!
They tell me that some child's been born
who'll take my kingdom and my crown!
Some mother's son, some father's brat
will be a king! I won't have that!
The thought fills me with dread and fear!
There's only room for one king here!
And what's more, before I'm done,
there will still be just the one.
Which is me, for I propose,
to kill this child before it grows.

There's just one thing wrong with this plan,
though they've tried, nobody can
discover where this brat is hid.
That won't stop me, I'll still be rid

of him, for here's what I will do –
kill all the children under two.
That way, I can be sure this child,
with all the others, will be killed,
the threat removed with one swift blow –
it's drastic action, yes, I know,
but for such an ill, you must agree,
this is the only remedy.

I'll give the order straight away
that, with the dawning of the day,
all children will be rounded up
and slaughtered – just like drowning pups.
No one will blame me. After all,
it's really only pest control,
the quickest, and the best solution
for keeping down the population.
And when the job's been carried out
I'll have a feast, to celebrate,

and each invited guest can sing
my praises – Herod, the only king!

HEROD goes.

Three MOTHERS enter.

1ST MOTHER Sunrise comes, a new day dawning,
glistening cold this winter's morning –

2ND MOTHER Fires are lit, the breakfast's cooking,
on the stove, the kettle's singing –

3RD MOTHER Drink your tea, and put your clothes on,
wash your face, and draw the curtain –

ALL It's a day like any other.

1ST MOTHER In the streets the women gather,
shivering in the chilly weather –

2ND MOTHER Washing windows, scrubbing doorsteps,

swapping all the latest gossip –

3RD MOTHER All the latest news and scandal,
while the children play and tumble –

ALL It's a day like any other.

The MOTHERS speak as if to their children.

1ST MOTHER Can't you play a little quieter?
Must you kneel down in the gutter?

2ND MOTHER Look! You've got your trousers dirty!
Wipe your nose! And use a hanky!

3RD MOTHER See the state you've got yourself in!
Get inside! And no complaining!

ALL It's a day like any other.

They speak to each other.

1ST MOTHER Kids! You wonder why you bother!
First it's one thing, then another!

2ND MOTHER Up your skirts and round your ankles,
nothing but a load of trouble!

3RD MOTHER All the fuss and all the rumpus!
All the pain and grief they bring us!

ALL It's a day like any other.

1ST MOTHER But there isn't any doubting
that we wouldn't be without them –

2ND MOTHER Worth the worry and the weeping,
worth it all, ours for the keeping –

3RD MOTHER Ours to love and care and nurture,
flesh and blood, our hope and future.

ALL It's a day like any other.

CAPTAIN enters and speaks to the women.

CAPTAIN Ladies! Your attention, please!
I've something to tell you, and you won't find it pleasant,
so I won't mince my words, and come straight to the point.
I have an order here,
written and signed by King Herod himself,
and by this order
your children are condemned to die,
the sentence to be carried out this morning.
It's not all your children whose lives must be taken,
only the little ones, those under two.
The rest, who are older, you can keep.
Don't ask the reason for it. Herod has his reasons,
and they must be for the greater good.
Don't protest or cry out
or try to prevent us from doing what we're here to do –
you know it won't do any good.
As far as you're concerned, your children are already dead.
They were dead the moment this order was signed.
Think of it, if you like, as a natural disaster,
storm or drought or plague,
something you have absolutely no control over –
an act of God.
Let's face it, as far as we're all concerned,
that's just what Herod is –
a mortal god who strikes where he wants,
and right now he's decided to strike down your children.
So give them up to us,
hand them over and go into your homes,
shut your doors and windows tight
so you won't see or hear what happens.
Believe me, it'll be better that way,
better for all of us, that way, believe me.

While he has been speaking, three SOLDIERS have entered, standing behind the MOTHERS, unseen by them. The CAPTAIN now addresses these SOLDIERS.

Right, lads.

You've got your orders.
Carry them out.

The MOTHERS turn as if to run, but each one finds herself confronted by a SOLDIER. The SOLDIERS mime killing the children as they speak.

1ST MOTHER Have mercy, please!

1ST SOLDIER There's no use crying.

2ND MOTHER Spare my child!

2ND SOLDIER He's bound for dying.

3RD MOTHER Show pity!

3RD SOLDIER I don't know that word.

1ST MOTHER My baby!

1ST SOLDIER He'll dance on my sword.

2ND MOTHER But why?

2ND SOLDIER For my king and country

3RD MOTHER God curse you all!

3RD SOLDIER Then cursed we'll be.

The MOTHERS bow their heads.

CAPTAIN That's it, lads.
You've done your duty.
Move out, now.

The SOLDIERS go. CAPTAIN speaks to the audience.

Don't ask me to justify this.
I can't.
I'm just a soldier, carrying out orders.
It's my job, what I'm trained for,
and I do it, no matter how dirty it is sometimes,
and sometimes, like now, it gets very dirty...

I didn't join the army to kill children,
and I don't pretend I like doing it,
but orders are orders,
and if it wasn't me carried them out, it would've been somebody else
and the end result would have been the same...
I'm a family man,
I've got a wife, children of my own,
and I daresay I'll have some bad nights over this,
but they'll pass,
because you can't let yourself think about it,
you have to shut yourself off from it,
just see it as a job to be done,
that's the only way to survive,
follow your orders, do your duty,
and try to live with honour and dignity.
Duty, honour and dignity –
if you don't have them,
what else have you got?

Yes, I'll have some bad nights,
some very bad nights over this,
but they'll pass...
they always pass.

The CAPTAIN goes. The MOTHERS turn back to the audience.

1ST MOTHER Now the sky bleeds light and sorrow,
now with grief our hearts are harrowed –

2ND MOTHER See our children's bodies broken,
see this death that has awoken –

3RD MOTHER Stalked our streets with wrath and cruelty,
left the world silent and empty –

1ST MOTHER Where mothers walk and weep and cry –

2ND MOTHER And pity kneels with blinded eyes –

3RD MOTHER And tyrants rule, and children die.

ALL
On this day –
On this day –
On this day that's like no other.

MOTHERS go.

HEROD enters.

HEROD
It's done! The deed's been carried out!
Now I've reason to celebrate,
my throne and crown again secure,
and Herod king for evermore! 23
And so it is I've feasted well,
eaten hearty, drunk my fill
of rich, red wines and dishes rare,
food and drink beyond compare,
indulging every appetite
from early morning through till night,
till my stomach's swollen wide –
and now I've got this pain inside!

My gut's on fire! A sword flame
stabs through it! There it goes again! 24
See how it's bloated with the load
I've gorged – I fear it will explode!
Oh, God! Oh, heaven! Oh, hell and grief!
It can't go on! I need relief!
Oh! The agony and pain!
No matter how I heave and strain,
this solid blockage in my gut
just won't come out! It's staying put!
I need a doctor! I feel sick!

DEATH enters. 25

DEATH
Here I am.

HEROD
What? That was quick!

DEATH
I couldn't help but hear you shout,
so here I am to help you out.
You have a blockage, so I've heard.

HEROD Can you move it?

DEATH Here's my word.

HEROD Are you certain?

DEATH Rest assured,
When I cure people, they stay cured.

HEROD Then hurry up! It's getting worse!
I feel like I'm about to burst!

DEATH Don't worry, Herod, I'll soon fix
you good and proper, and no tricks,
no secret spells, no midnight magic,
no linctus, drugs, or paregoric.
My medicine cures all men's ills,
it's simple, plain, no fuss nor frills,
much better than a box of pills,
it's older than the oldest hills,
soothes and relaxes you, until
you're lying stiff and cold and still,
for it not only cures, it kills –

HEROD Your words have made my blood run chill!
My hair stands up! I'm short of breath!
Who are you? Tell me!

DEATH I am Death.
I come and go just as I please,
softer than the softest breeze.
And when that breeze begins to blow,
it fills your heart with ice and snow.
And when that snow begins to fall,
then swoops on silent wings the owl.
And when that owl begins to shriek,
you feel the biting of its beak.
And when that bite begins to hurt,
it's like a knifeblade in your heart.
And when your heart begins to bleed,
then you are dead, and mine indeed.

HEROD I won't die! Hear what I said? 29

DEATH Herod, you're already dead.
You died about an hour since,
around the time you took the last mince-
tart and stuffed it down your neck –
it wouldn't budge, and there it stuck.
You coughed and spluttered, gasped for breath –
then fell face forward, choked to death.
Now I'm here to grip you by the hand,
And send you down to hell's dark land.

HEROD Have mercy, please! 30

DEATH It's no use crying.

HEROD Spare my life!

DEATH You're bound for dying.

HEROD Show pity!

DEATH I don't know that word.

HEROD My soul!

DEATH Will dance on the devil's sword.

Three DEVILS emerge from Hell's mouth and surround HEROD. DEATH turns and goes.

1ST DEVIL Hold him fast! No more delay! 31
It's time to take this wretch away!

2ND DEVIL As Herod is this villain's name,
we'll roast him in tormenting flames!

3RD DEVIL For he's a sinner most complete,
and fit, therefore, to be our meat!

1ST DEVIL A host of children died today,
and not one soul did come our way.

2ND DEVIL Up to heaven they've all gone,
and we've been left with just this one.

3RD DEVIL And all our rage and wrath and spite
we'll pour on him, for our delight!

1ST DEVIL Nine circles are there down in hell,
and in the deepest one he'll dwell.

2ND DEVIL Howling, weeping in his grief,
but he'll never have relief.

3RD DEVIL Bound in red-hot, burning wires,
to suffer in eternal fires!

They take hold of HEROD. HEROD cries out in terror. They drag him down into Hell's mouth.

MARY enters, carrying JESUS.

MARY We left town in the dead of night,
like fugitives, took flight
along a dark and lonely road,
not knowing where it would lead,
or if our wandering would ever end.
Now we live far from family or friend,
strangers in a foreign land,
and why we must, is something I don't understand.

Child in my arms,
what hate or harm
could ever the world wish to you?
Yet it seems that it's so,
and that you were born
for suffering and pain,
and woe.
For on that night
when I cradled you tight
in my arms
a circle of light
deadly bright
danced around your head
sharp as steel thorns,

and your weight
in my arms
was like that of the dead.
I was filled with such dread,
and still am.

You look at me, eyes full of trust,
but in my mouth's the taste of dust.
Your smile's sweetness stings my heart,
and fills my soul with grief and hurt.
And your lips upon my breast
drive like nails through my chest,
pinning me against the tree
of some future agony.

And now I know there's more to birth
than the smiles of joy and mirth,
and I know too there's more to death,
than mere stopping of the breath.
And love itself a mystery
that binds your life and death to me.

Little child, your hand I'll take,
and give to you my heart to break,
for a mother's love is like the sea,
deep, and flowing endlessly.

In this I put my faith and trust
and hope, because I know I must.
So we'll go on, and not look back,
but fix our feet to the outward track.

MARY goes.

END OF THE SEVENTH PLAY

4 The Crucifixion and the Resurrection

Three SOLDIERS enter, carrying a large wooden cross. They lay it down as they speak.

1st SOLDIER Who's this they're sending us today
to put to death. Eh, have you heard?

2nd SOLDIER Some kind of rebel, so they say.

1st SOLDIER An agitator?

2nd SOLDIER That's the word
out on the streets.

1st SOLDIER One of that crew!
I hate the lot – a waste of breath
is what they are, I'm telling you
that we should put them all to death.
Hang the whole bleeding lot,
string them up from the tree
and there let them rot
for the whole world to see.

3rd SOLDIER I heard that he's a holy man,
a wonder-worker.

2nd SOLDIER Is that right?

3rd SOLDIER Yes. One of those, you know who can
cure the lame and bring back sight
to blind men.

1st SOLDIER What? And raise the dead?

3rd SOLDIER They say he has.

1st SOLDIER I bet they do!
And that he's the Son of God,
the new Messiah! It's all true!

3RD SOLDIER That's the claim that some make.

1ST SOLDIER Take note of me, brother,
this one's a fake,
just like all the others.

2ND SOLDIER Do you know this prophet's name?

3RD SOLDIER Jesus – well, that's how it's spoke
in Greek –

2ND SOLDIER Oh, yes? I've heard of him!
He's some crazy kind of a bloke,
a wild man from the wilderness,
telling all the folks to leave
and follow him.

3RD SOLDIER Where to?

1ST SOLDIER My guess
is all the way into the grave.
'Cos that's where he's bound.

2ND SOLDIER I think you speak true.
He'll be under the ground
before this day's through.

1ST SOLDIER I've come across his kind before.
They're two-a-penny. There was one
made all the headlines just last year.
You remember – name of John.

3RD SOLDIER That roaring ranter. He could go
for hours, preaching of doom and fate.
What happened to him?

1ST SOLDIER Don't you know?
They served his head up on a plate.

2ND SOLDIER All these agitators
must be sick in the head,
'cos sooner or later
they all end up dead.

1ST SOLDIER

A good thing too. Them holy shakers
are the last thing people want.
Good-for-nothing troublemakers,
stirring strife and discontent.
This one's no different to the rest,
so string him up and watch him die.
You'll find that when he breathes his last,
there won't be nobody to cry.
He'll be gone and forgot
in an hour or two,
left to lie and to rot –

Another SOLDIER enters, calling out.

4TH SOLDIER

Dead man coming through!

Behind the 4TH SOLDIER comes JESUS, hands bound, followed by a 5TH SOLDIER.

Here he is, all tied and trussed,
just like a lamb for the knife.

1ST SOLDIER

(To Jesus.) Come on, lad, you've walked your last,
you're destined now for death and dust.
It's time to end your life.

2ND SOLDIER

Got the order?

5TH SOLDIER

Here you are,
all signed and sealed.

2ND SOLDIER

Okay.
Have any trouble getting here?

5TH SOLDIER

None at all.

3RD SOLDIER

You ready there?
We don't want no delay.

2ND SOLDIER

I'm coming!

1ST SOLDIER

Good. Take up your tools,
there's a job that's got to be done.

An execution takes some skill,
it ain't no piece of cake to kill
a man, so let's get on.

All becomes still as JESUS turns and speaks to the audience.

JESUS

And now my foretold agony begins,
now I'm prepared to suffer for the sins
of humankind. I'll bear upon my back
the load of human misery, and crack
my heart and die an innocent man's death,
and let my sinless bones be crushed beneath
earth's rock and weight.
For this fate I was born,
and made to wear life like a crown of thorns,
to break the lock and link of Adam's chains
forged by Lucifer, and by mankind worn
these weary centuries. Look upon me,
fashioned to suffer for humanity,
for when I'm nailed and hanging from the tree,
my death-shout will cry out their liberty.

The action begins again.

1ST SOLDIER Untie his hands first.

3RD SOLDIER Understood.

1ST SOLDIER Now stand on either side.
Got him secure?

2ND SOLDIER We have.

1ST SOLDIER That's good.
Now lay him down upon the wood
and stretch his arms out wide.

The SOLDIERS lay JESUS down on the cross.

4TH SOLDIER About the crowd, what do you say?
Shall I let them through?

1ST SOLDIER No fear.
We don't want any more delay.

4TH SOLDIER I've got you. I'll keep them at bay
till he's hanging in the air.

5TH SOLDIER To think, that till a while ago,
he couldn't do no wrong.
He was their lord of life, but now
they want the blood of their Holy Joe,
and they sing a different song.

4TH SOLDIER The crowd needs to be entertained
and it don't care much how.
It ain't an animal with brains,
it just wants blood and death and pain.
I mean, look at it now.

Pause.

See them faces staring in –

5TH SOLDIER You can almost smell their breath.

4TH SOLDIER Those bloodshot eyes, those leering grins –
They can't wait for it to begin,
They've got the taste of death.

1ST SOLDIER Got your nails?

2ND SOLDIER They're sharp and bright.

3RD SOLDIER See how they gleam and shine.

1ST SOLDIER Knock them in both hard and tight.

2ND SOLDIER I'll take the left hand.

3RD SOLDIER Me, the right.

1ST SOLDIER His feet, then, they'll be mine.

3RD SOLDIER I'll hammer this straight through in one.

2ND SOLDIER It'll take you three or four!

3RD SOLDIER You reckon?

2ND SOLDIER Lay your money down!

3RD SOLDIER A wager is it? Right, you're on!
We'll soon settle this score.

1ST SOLDIER hammers in the nail.

3RD SOLDIER A single blow! Just like I said!
I knew I'd win this game.
I knocked it flush down to the head,
and now the blood flows dark and red –

2ND SOLDIER I bet I can do the same.

2ND SOLDIER hammers in the nail.

There's one!

3RD SOLDIER It's not gone through.

2ND SOLDIER I know.
There's two!

3RD SOLDIER It don't look straight.

2ND SOLDIER One more, and in!

3RD SOLDIER You took three blows.
I took just one. I win, you lose,
so give us my winnings, mate!

1ST SOLDIER Leave that till later. Is he fast?

2ND SOLDIER He's fixed and won't come free.

1ST SOLDIER His feet are firm, I'll put my trust
in that.

3RD SOLDIER Not till he's breathed his last
will he come off this tree.

1ST SOLDIER Time now to heave this cross upright,
and that's no easy task.

2ND SOLDIER We need some help.

3RD SOLDIER Why don't we ask
those two lads there? They'll lend their backs.

1ST SOLDIER I just had the same thought.
Hey lads! Come here and lend a hand
to lift this cross.

4TH SOLDIER Right-oh.
Tell us what to do and where to stand,
we'll help you all we can.

1ST SOLDIER That's grand.
Now we're all set to go.
Take hold of the cross as we haul on the ropes,
keep it steady and hold it fast.

5TH SOLDIER Like this?

1ST SOLDIER That's it, and keep a good grip,
and with effort and luck and a lot of hope
we'll have this cross up at last.

They raise the cross.

2ND SOLDIER Here goes, then, lads!

3RD SOLDIER Heave!

4TH SOLDIER Push!

1ST SOLDIER Take care!
Don't rush.

5TH SOLDIER It's slipping!

4TH SOLDIER Hold on!

1ST SOLDIER Just let each man do his share.

2ND SOLDIER One last effort, boys!

3RD SOLDIER It's there!

1ST SOLDIER Now that was a job well done.

The cross is standing now.

Now let him hang upon the tree,
while we must stand and wait,
and pass the time and watch as he
lets go his life in agony –
for that's his fate.

The SOLDIERS move to the back of the stage and stand guard. Two CHORUSES OF CITIZENS enter, also MARY, and MAGDALENA, who stand apart from the others.

CHORUS 1 There He is, look, there
There's the holy man
The prophet,
Hanging like a criminal from the cross.
This kind of death
This death reserved for thieves and murderers
This kind of death shouldn't be His.
Why this agonising and humiliating death for Him?
What's He done?
What crime has He committed?
What in the world has He done to deserve this?

CHORUS 2 What's he done?
We'll tell you what he's done
Blasphemy for a start!
Going round saying he was the son of God.
Blasphemy
That's a crime in this country
A capital crime
And he's guilty of it and he's paying the price.

CHORUS 1 So maybe he's a madman
Maybe he was deluded
Or just misguided
But he was just a preacher
A holy man

And maybe sometimes he went a bit too far
But is that any reason to kill him like this?

CHORUS 2
You think that's all he was?
A holy man? A preacher?
More fool you for being taken in
He was more than that
A crowd-stirrer
A rabble-rouser
Telling people to leave their families
Telling them to give away all their money
He wanted to destroy society
He wanted to turn the world upside-down
He was against everything we believe in
And he deserves everything that he's got.

MAGDALENA
How can you say that about him?
How can you say all those things?
He never did any wrong,
never harmed or hurt anyone,
He just talked about God,
spoke to the poor and the injured
the weak and the helpless
and told them how God loved them
That's what he talked about
Love
That's the thing that moved him,
that made him do and say
all the things he did and said
Love
I knew him, knew him as well as anyone
and that's all I ever saw in him
Love, only
Love

CHORUS 2
How dare you speak to us of love!
How dare you speak to us at all!
You

There's only one kind of love you've ever known
And that's the kind that's bought and sold
You
You and your kind
You're a disgrace to decent people
And you're the kind he mixed with
Whores and pimps and thieves
Beggars and outcasts and undesirables
You're all a cancer in society
String them all up, that's what we say
All the riff-raff and rubbish
Promised you the kingdom of heaven?
There's his kingdom!
Go and share it with him!
We'll be glad to be rid of you
You and all the rest.

CHORUS 1 I heard He cured the sick
He had the gift of healing
They followed Him everywhere
The blind and the crippled
The deaf and the mute
And He cured them
All life's casualties
Just a touch of His hand, they say
Just a word
And I heard too how He brought someone back from the dead
A man dead and buried
He brought him back to life
And if just half of what we've heard is true
How can we call this man a criminal?
How can we say it or even think it?
We're not saying we know who or what He was
But we're certain of this
He was a good man
And perhaps even touched by God

CHORUS 2

He was touched, all right
And so are you lot for letting yourselves get taken in
We've heard all those stories too
Miracles, wonder-cures
Walking on water and dancing on moonbeams
It's beyond us how anyone can believe in such nonsense
Come down out of the clouds
Put your feet on the ground
Live in the real world, not fairytale land
Miracles don't happen
The sick aren't cured by a kind word
The blind don't see
The dead don't walk
Look, look up there
There he is, your miracle-maker, hanging there, dying
If he can work wonders, why doesn't he work one now?
Why doesn't he get down off that cross?
Now that would be a miracle worth seeing
But we won't because he can't
He's no wonder-worker, no miracle-maker
Just a crowd-pleaser
A con-man with the gift of the gab
And though he might have fooled a few people
He's not fooling anyone now
We can all see him for what he is
Just a man
And all he can do is die

MAGDALENA

That's enough! Enough of this!
Think of his mother!
She's here, look, listening to what you're saying
No matter what you think of him,
no matter who or what you think he was
He was also her son
If you have no pity for him
have pity for her
It's enough she has to stand and watch him die this death

Don't make her torment any worse
Show pity
show mercy
and keep silent.

CHORUS 1
The woman's right
We should keep quiet now
We've all said enough
Perhaps too much
And look
He's dying
His strength's giving out
It won't be long now
Soon it will all be over
The end will come
And after that what is there to be said?

All stand still and silent now.

LUCIFER emerges from Hell's mouth.

LUCIFER
Now is my triumph and my victory!
To see the son of God pinned to the cross
and dying a criminal's death, it cheers
my withered heart to see him twist and writhe
in mortal agony. I am well pleased.

LUCIFER approaches JESUS on the cross and speaks to him.

Hey, you up there! Look down! Remember me?
I came to you when you were just a lad.
We met together on some mountain-top,
and there I offered you a gift. I said
you could be king of all the world, have fame,
wealth, glory, power – all you had to do
was recognise my right upon this earth.
But no, you turned your back, rejected me.
And why? For suffering humanity,
to save their souls and win them to God's grace.
And where's that got you? Nailed to this cross-tree,

abandoned by your followers, betrayed
by one of your own, and left here to hang, 38
carrion for crows. And where's your God?
Where's your almighty all-loving father
in your hour of need? I don't hear his voice.
All that I hear is silence. No one's there.
You're all alone. Above, just empty sky.
You've failed. I've won. And in that knowledge, die!

LUCIFER turns from JESUS and speaks to the audience.

Let earth wither, let sky and sun turn black,
for when he dies, the devil's on his back!

LUCIFER descends into Hell's mouth. 39

1ST SOLDIER Okay, brave lads, now get back to your posts,
I reckon he's about to breathe his last.
And one of us, now that he's near his end,
must stick him with a spear, and so we'll send
his soul to hell, or heaven, or nowhere –

JESUS cries out from the cross.

JESUS My father!

1ST SOLDIER Ah! That gave me quite a scare!
To hear him cry out put the wind up me –

JESUS cries out again. 40

JESUS My father! Why have you forsaken me?

2ND SOLDIER He cries again – his voice lone and forlorn,
as if regretting he was ever born.

3RD SOLDIER So he must. It's a bad ending, all right.
I'm almost moved to pity at the sight.

4TH SOLDIER He called out for his father.

5TH SOLDIER It's a cry
that men make when they know they're going to die.

They want someone to ease their fear and pain,
for in their hearts they are children again.

2ND SOLDIER There's something in his voice that I don't like.
It pierces me right through, sharp as a spike
driven through my heart.

1ST SOLDIER Come on, now, lads!
We ain't young kids. We know that dying's bad,
we've seen it all before, and will again,
so let's to business and get this thing done
and finished with. Who'll volunteer
to end his life?

2ND SOLDIER Not me.

3RD SOLDIER Nor me, I fear.

4TH SOLDIER Our job was just to bring him to the top
of this hill, and that's where our duties stop.

5TH SOLDIER We've done more than we should already, so
it's time we left you, and went back below
to barracks. We've got other duties there
to see to. You can see to yours up here.

4TH and 5TH SOLDIERS go.

1ST SOLDIER It's up to one of us, then. But which one?
Looks like it falls to me to get it done.

He speaks to 2ND SOLDIER.

Give me your spear. I'll finish him. And then
our duty's done –

JESUS Father!

2ND SOLDIER He cries again!
A voice that tears my soul –

JESUS Into your care
I give my spirit!

3RD SOLDIER Look, boys! See, up there!
The sun's turned black! 44

2ND SOLDIER And listen! Do you hear?
The sound of wailing voices fills the air!

1ST SOLDIER It's just the wind –

2ND SOLDIER It's not. It's something more!
I never heard wind howl like that before!

3RD SOLDIER And what's that noise that shakes the ground beneath?

2ND SOLDIER The earth itself cries out for this man's death!

1ST SOLDIER There's something strange, all right. More than we know.

2ND SOLDIER I fear to stay.

3RD SOLDIER I think that we should go 45
and get out while we can.

2ND SOLDIER I'm with you there.

1ST SOLDIER We can't just leave his body hanging there!

2ND SOLDIER We can.

3RD SOLDIER And will. He said he was God's son.
If God's his father, he can fetch him down!

The three SOLDIERS go.

The 1ST CHORUS now approach the cross. As they speak, they take JESUS' body down.

CHORUS 1 He promised us eternal life 46
But life has been cut short for Him
He said He'd lead us to the kingdom of heaven
If we listened to His words and followed Him
We listened
We followed
And this is where He led us
Here

To this hill of skulls
This kingdom of death

We believed he was the son of God
And if he was the son of God
Why bring us to this place?
All we see here is death
And perhaps that's what he wanted
All his life moving towards this one final act
Forcing us to stare death in the face
Making his death ours
All our deaths made one and happening here
On this bare hilltop
Today and now

So the cold wind that blows
Blows through our bones
And the voices that wail
Are our own ghost-voices
And the darkness that descends and blots out the sun
Is the darkness that each one of us carries within us
And the dryness in our mouths
Is the taste of dust
And this body that we carry
Is the dead weight of our own mortal flesh
And its stillness and its silence
Are the stillness and silence that lie under our tongues
Unable to speak any longer
Or utter sound.

JESUS' body lies on the floor, now. The CHORUS steps back as MARY approaches him. She kneels beside him, lifts him, cradles him, as she speaks.

MARY
This is my son –
This was my son –
This was the child – the man –
This is his body.

Little child, your hand I'll take,
and give to you my heart to break,
for a mother's love is like the sea...

Once he was playing outside, and he fell and cut his knee, and he came into the house crying and I bathed his wound and washed the blood away and then I wiped the tears from his face and held him in my arms until the pain was gone and he smiled again...

No more... 51

I hold him in my arms and he's cold
I hold him and his coldness flows into me,
a river of coldness flooding my body,
pouring through every vein and fibre
and I become numb
I feel nothing
I have become stone,
cold, hard stone
I am a stone tomb enveloping him
my heart is the rock rolled across the black doorway 52
my body is the hollowed-out cave in which he lies

the cold womb from which he will never be born.

MARY rises and moves away to stand near MAGDALENA. The CHORUS slowly gather round JESUS' body, hiding him from view.

CHORUS 1

Sun sinks
Day ends
Deeper darkness
Now descends

Night passes
Grief-torn 53
Bitter tears
Greet the dawn

Empty eyes
Greet the light
This day passes
Into night

And there's no
Relief from pain
Soon the day
Will dawn again

And so we wait
Through fading night
To greet once more
The risen light.

MAGDALENA And as that new sun rises in the sky,
we look – and we cannot believe our eyes –
For there, in the clear, shining light of day,
we see the stone that blocked the tomb has now been rolled away.

The CHORUS now part, to reveal that Jesus' body is no longer there.

MARY In fear we enter into that grim cave,
which up till now has been my dead son's grave,
and find to our amazement nothing there –
and shimmering light and scent of flowers fills the morning air.

JESUS enters behind MARY and MAGDALENA.

JESUS Why do you weep? Why do you cry?
The sun is risen in the sky,
and I am risen from the tomb,
for death itself has met its doom.

MARY and MAGDALENA turn and see JESUS.

They hung me on a wooden cross,
and put death's mask upon my face,
but if the spirit's pure, then death can't win,
and life just bounces back again.

I went where all the stars turn black,
I had the devil on my back,
but I shook him off and threw him down,
and all hell shivered with the sound.

See where the nails went in my hands,
look, believe, and understand,
this is the gift I bring to you,
Adam's flesh, re-made anew,

This is the reason for my life
and death, to bring an end to strife.
Where I stand all life begins
again, set free from fear and sin.

Now every girl and every boy
may live in everlasting joy,
and each woman and each man
dwell in the human form divine

whose flesh is of pure beaten gold,
and can't be bought and can't be sold,
and walks in wonder and delight
and shines with heaven's purest light.

GOD appears above.

GOD

My work is now completed, and made whole,
now love can blossom in the human soul,
unfettered by the chains of that first crime
which was committed at the start of time,
when Lucifer himself sought to destroy
all I had made. Now all is bliss and joy,
for humankind is freed at last from fear
of death, and my creation shines out clear.
As mist clears from a hilltop and reveals
the shimmering landscape – valleys, rivers, fields
illuminated by a golden light,
the universe now shines out pure and bright.

Lift up your eyes, and let your spirits soar
beyond the burning stars, through heaven's door,
embrace the world as it was meant to be
and live and thrive and grow eternally.

End of the Final Play

Looking back at the plays

Staging the plays

The production of the Mystery Plays in the Middle Ages was spectacular. The wagons on which the plays were staged were brightly decorated, and the sets themselves often highly complicated and elaborate. For example, there were moving clouds that parted to reveal God; golden wheels that spun to represent the universe; machinery for lifting actors up to heaven; a great, open mouth from which flames and smoke belched to depict hell; huge copper sheets were beaten, or wooden drums filled with stones were revolved to create the sound of thunder; and, in the Coventry cycle, three worlds were constructed for the Last Judgement, and burned during the performance to depict the end of creation.

Choose one of the plays in this book, and create or design the set and props for its production. Make them as spectacular as you can, but remember that they must also work, be practical, and safe! You could possibly do this work in pairs, with one of you describing the set and props, and the other making drawings of them. If you wish, you could also try making a small working model of the set.

Imagine you are one of the townsfolk present at a staging of the Mystery Plays in your town. Describe the performance of one of the more spectacular plays. It may well be that people you know are acting in the play, and you may have helped to build the set or make the props. In your writing, try and create a real sense of wonder and excitement as you describe all you see, hear and feel.

Speaking the plays

The plays in *Heaven and Earth*, like the original medieval plays, are for the most part written in verse. With its rhythmic lines and rhymes, verse is easier to memorise than prose.

Choose a rhymed speech from one of the plays and try memorising it, and then speaking it aloud. You'll probably find it easier to break the speech up into smaller sections, and memorise each section individually before you go on to the next. How long does it take you to become word-perfect? What is it about the speech that makes it most easy to memorise – the rhythm of the lines, or the rhyme? Now try doing the same with one of the unrhymed (blank verse) speeches. Is that as easy to memorise, or more difficult?

Different verse-forms were used in the original plays, and I've used different verse-forms in my plays. Here are a few examples:

a) Behold my throne, lit by eternal light,
The symbol of my majesty and might.
And all about it, let angels appear,
The guardians and spirits of the spheres.

(Regular rhythm, ten syllables to each line. Paired lines rhyme.)

b) Where is she? Where's that woman of mine?
Where's the wench that I'm bound to wed?
I've looked everywhere,
But can't find hide nor hair,
And there's something between us that needs to be said.

(Verse of 5 lines; lines 2 and 5 rhyme with each other; lines 3 and 4 rhyme with each other. Lines 3 and 4 are shorter than lines 1, 2 and 5.)

c) Who'd be a shepherd on a night like this?
Not me if I could help it, but I can't.
Born to it, I was, just as my poor dad
was before me, and all our wretched kind,
all the way back to Adam, damn his eyes!

(Lines have regular rhythm of ten syllables each, but there is no rhyme at the end.)

d) This one's no different to the rest,
so string him up and watch him die.
You'll find that when he breathes his last,
there won't be nobody to cry.

(Verses in groups of four lines. Lines 1 and 3 rhyme with each other, lines 2 and 4 rhyme with each other.)

See what other verse-forms you can find in the plays, write down examples of them, and give a brief description of each one, as above.

Choose three or four of these different verse-forms, and try writing a few lines of your own in each form. Which do you find the easiest to write, and which the most difficult? Can you say why?

Speaking dialogue in verse can be a little tricky if you haven't done it before. You need to keep to the rhythm of the verse, but at the same time make the dialogue sound as natural as you can. This means not letting either the rhythm or the rhyme be too obvious, but making sure they're still present.

In groups of 2, 3 or 4, choose a section from one of the plays where dialogue is being spoken using a verse-form. Have a go at speaking it to each other until you feel it sounds right – that is, until it sounds both like verse and like dialogue. It might feel rather awkward at first, but after a few attempts it will become more and more natural to you.

In the first play, the lines of God and the Angels are spoken in verse that has regular rhythm and rhyme, but those of Lucifer are irregular. Why do you think this is? What do you think the kinds of language they speak are telling us about the characters? Can you find examples in any of the other plays, where the language or verse-form used by a character tells us something about that character?

Character

Characters in the Mystery Plays tend to be quite simply drawn – usually they're either Good or Bad. This is because the original plays were written with a religious message, showing people how they should behave, and what might happen to them if they didn't follow God. I didn't write my plays with any religious message in mind, so I did try to make some of the characters a little more complex. For example, although Cain is a murderer, and therefore a 'bad' character who must be punished, Abel is rather smug and self-righteous, and Cain is partly justified in thinking that his mother loves Abel more. This isn't saying that Cain's murder of Abel is right, but that there may be more than one simple reason for it.

Try going through the plays making a list of all the 'good' characters and a list of all the 'bad' characters. Are there any characters you find difficult to put into the two lists? Take Adam and Eve, for example. What they do – disobeying God – should be regarded as bad, but are they actually 'bad' people? And are there are 'good' characters who aren't perhaps all good?

If you are acting a character in a play, it's helpful to try to understand something about that character – to imagine how they might speak and think about themselves. One way of doing this is to write a short monologue for that character, letting the character talk about events from his or her point of view. Here are a few suggestions:

a) Cain trying to explain why he killed his brother.
b) One of the Wicked from 'The Flood' saying what he or she thinks about Noah building his ship.
c) Mary's Mother or Father saying how they feel about discovering their daughter is having a child.
d) Mak or Sal trying to justify their stealing of the lamb.
e) One of the soldiers who took part in the 'Slaughter of the Innocents', saying how he feels after the event.

There are many other possibilities.

After you have chosen your character, read through the play where she or he appears before you start writing. Keep your writing simple and direct, trying to hear in your own mind the sound of the character's voice, and what she or he is saying.

More Mysteries

Some time ago, I wrote modern versions of several of the Mystery Plays, taking the general themes behind the plays, and putting them into a different setting. My version of the Noah play was about an amateur radio broadcaster who hears the voice of God over his radio. God commands the broadcaster to build a massive radio receiver in his back garden so that God can broadcast a message to the whole world. The broadcaster does this, but in doing so, angers his neighbours, the council, the police, and his own wife. Eventually he's arrested and taken away.

You could try writing your own modern version of one of the plays in this book. First of all, choose the play you'd like to re-write, then summarise briefly what happens in it, and what it's about, for instance like this:

Story: There are two brothers, Cain and Abel. Cain is jealous of Abel and kills him. His crime is discovered and he runs away.

Themes: Jealousy, rivalry between brothers, punishment.

Once you've done this, forget the story of the original play, and just concentrate on the themes. See if you can create a new story from the themes. Once you've worked out your new story, then you can try turning that into a short play. You can either write it, or improvise it in groups.

Religion in the Middle Ages

To understand how the Mystery Plays came to be written, you need to understand a little about how people thought in the Middle Ages, and what they believed. In England, as in most of Europe, the Christian religion was one of the most important things in people's lives, and the Church was a powerful and wealthy organisation. Using books and CD-ROMs, see what you can find out about religion and the Church in the Middle Ages, and how central it was to people's lives and beliefs.